BOOM TOWNS
& RELIC HUNTERS
OF NORTHEASTERN WASHINGTON

A Comprehensive Guide to Ghost Towns
in Six Historic Counties

By Jerry Smith

Elfin Cove Press

1481 130th Avenue NE

Bellevue, WA 98005

www.elfincovepress.com

Project manager: Bernie Kuntz

Text and Cover Design: Amy Peloff

Editor: Lisa McCoy

ISBN 0944958-28-1

Printed in the United States of America

1 3 5 7 9 10 8 6 4 2

DEDICATION

"Smitty"

*To my father and best friend, Lloyd E. Smith (1921-1996), who took me to
Winthrop at the age of 13 to see and explore the mountains and valleys of Okanogan
country in search of those ghost towns of yesteryear. Thanks, Dad!*

⚷⚸⚹⚺⚻⚼⚽⚾⚿⛀⛁⛂⛃⛄⛅⛆⛇⛈⛉⛊⛋⛌⛍⛎⛏⛐⛑⛒⛓⛔⛕⛖
⛗⛘⛙⛚⛛⛜⛝⛞⛟⛠⛡⛢⛣⛤⛥⛦⛧⛨⛩⛪⛫⛬⛭⛮⛯

*These frontier branding iron symbols represent the initials of the author's family members. Seems like there's some-
thing adventurous and dramatic about an old branding iron. Perhaps it's because the iron is a sort of personal
monogram, an owner's mark, a kind of coat of arms of the Wild West Frontier Americana.*

TABLE OF CONTENTS

Important Notice

Disclaimer of Trespass

The land on which many of the ghost towns presented in this book are on is private land and strictly off-limits for entry except by permission only.

Please do not trespass WITHOUT PERMISSION IN WRITING from those in authority owning the land.

Disclaimer of Liability

The author, publisher, staff, and any and all associates or partners of this book do not endorse, condone, or suggest illegal trespassing onto private property or Native American lands presented in this book. We do not accept liability for those who trespass onto lands presented in this book.

We do not accept liability for any loss or injury to persons or property as a result of content written in this book. Trespassing and acquiring entry permission onto lands mentioned in this book, as well as personal safety, are solely the responsibility of any and all persons visiting lands mentioned in this book. This disclaimer is considered a fair and reasonable warning and notice to those who visit said lands.

A bird's-eye view looking south down Main Street Riverside Avenue in downtown Winthrop in its early years. The largest building in the center of the photo was Guy Waring's Methow Trading Company, which was located on the corner where Sheri's Sweet Shop is today. The Winthrop Hotel can be seen in the right center of the picture and remains today as the renowned Winthrop Palace. The Duck Brand Saloon in the left center of the photo stands today as the present town hall and Winthrop Chamber of Commerce visitor/information center. (Photo from Okanogan County Historical Society collection).

ACKNOWLEDGMENTS

I would like to acknowledge Washington's early-day pioneers, miners, prospectors, and Native American people. Without them and their accomplishments, we would have none of this history. These pioneers had the courage and strong will that was a match for this rugged yet fascinating land. Also, to those descendants of pioneer families that are still part of the life of Okanogan country today, who have shared their recollections with me.

Special thanks to my nephew, Jim O'Brien, Web master and designer of our Web site "Boom Towns & Relic Hunters of Northeastern Washington State," for his guidance and direction. Thanks especially to my wife Laurie and my son Cody for their understanding and patience.

Special Individual Contributors

Rob Stone
The Old Town of Nighthawk
Gold Hill
Nighthawk Mining Claims Turn to Riches

Pauline Strickler Crane
Pioneers of Springdale

Loretta Louis
Ruby City: The Life and Death of a Mining Town

Bruce A. Wilson
Okanogan County's Mysterious "China Wall"
More About David McLaughlin, The Man in Charge

Kjell Lester
Hart's Pass Area History

Mabel Gavin
Old Loup Loup: The Lost City

Books

Okanogan County Heritage. Okanogan County Historical Society, Quarterly Publication, Okanogan, WA.

Trails & Tales of the Early Day Settlers of Northeast Okanogan County. Compiled by Wauconda & Surrounding Area Historical Committee.

Okanogan Highland Album. Compiled by Molson-Chewsaw-Knob Hill Community Development Committee. Printed by Statesman-Examiner, Inc. Colville, WA.

Late Frontier. Bruce A. Wilson. Okanogan County Historical Society, Okanogan, WA, 1990.

Program of Mining Research. U.S. Department of Health and Human Services.

Geology and Mining Information. Marshall Y. Huntting. Washington State Department of Natural Resources, a division of Geology and Earth Resources. Olympia, WA.

Inventory of Washington Minerals. Marshall T. Huntting.

Okanogan Highland Echoes. Compiled by Molson-Chewsaw-Knob Hill Community Development Committee. Printed by Statesman-Examiner, Inc. Colville, WA, 1986.

Geologic Time: Rocks, Fossils, and Minerals in Washington. State of Washington Department of Natural Resources, a division of Mines and Geology.

Historical Societies

Molson Historical Society
Shafer Museum
Okanogan County Historical Society

INTRODUCTION

Boom Towns & Relic Hunters of Northeastern Washington State is designed for use by anyone with an interest in the history of Northeastern Washington and the willingness to wander the roads of Okanogan country in search of the history of yesteryear.

This research represents an intriguing look back into Northeastern Washington's Gold Rush days of miners, prospectors, pioneers, Native Americans and ghost towns. This history revolves around the six historic mining counties of Northeastern Washington: Chelan, Kittitas, Ferry, Stevens, Pend Oreille, and Okanogan, which is the largest county in Washington State. In these six historic counties exist some of the most irresistible and historic regions in this state.

As a young boy, my father regularly brought me here fishing, hunting, camping, and exploring. Ever since those early years of my childhood, the beauty and tranquility of this country has inspired me. When the history of this country beckoned me, I began to explore and research more about the miners, prospectors, pioneers, and the old ghost towns.

I talked to local folks from around my area of Winthrop—some being pioneers in their days and descendents of these pioneers—as well as volunteers from local historical museums in the surrounding areas. Everyone that I talked to was very knowledgeable, helpful, and enjoyed sharing old stories. I searched through historical archives, read many books, and old articles, and looked at hundreds of historic photos during my many years of research.

Then, I struck out to explore and locate these relics from the past. Places like Ruby City, Loup Loup City, the Mysterious "China Wall," Fourth of July Mine, First Thought Mine, and Arlington Mine on Ruby Hill. Places like the lost mining camp of Okanogan City and Alder Mine, which produced over 1 million dollars in ore in its days. Many of these mines over a century ago produced millions of dollars in gold and silver ore, as other miners and prospectors continued to search the hills and mountains for their "glory hole."

So if you're not looking to strike it rich, but would like to revisit those colorful boomtown days of yesteryear and relive some of Washington's history, excitement is just waiting for you in historic Northeastern Washington State. For those of you whose history goes back far enough, I hope our book rekindles some of your memories.

Happy Trails!
Jerry Smith

WELCOME TO NORTHEASTERN WASHINGTON STATE

Welcome to Northeastern Washington—a rugged yet fascinating part of Washington State that is rich in history of the Old West mining era and so vividly echoes the memories of a time of boomtowns and million-dollar mines.

Many people imagine Washington as a rainy, cold place with lush rain forests, glaciated volcanoes, and tall evergreens with most of the population occupied by latté drinking aerospace and computer nerds. In fact, Washington is in many ways a place of two worlds.

While much of western Washington meets the above description pretty well, the east side of the state is rather different. Separated by the majestic Cascade Mountain Range, eastern Washington is arid, warm and reminiscent of the Wild, Wild West. Tumbleweeds, canyons, coyote, and free-range cattle pass you by as you drive the lonesome highways of the east. Stampedes, rodeos, and other Wild West traditions are still the way of life throughout much of this part of the country. So the next time you hear people talk about Washington State, remember us cowboys!

When gold fever struck the American West during the late 1800s, the Okanogan and the Methow Valley shone as a middle link in a glittering, beckoning chain that stretched from California to Alaska.

In 1849, a strike at Sutter's Mill in the Sierras kindled the gold mining frenzy. Ten years later, the procession of gold seekers trudged north through Northeastern Washington headed for rumored riches in Canada's caribou country. Many looked for a likely lode along the way. By the late 1890s, the quest had led most prospectors farther north to the Yukon Territory.

Some Okanogan stragglers succeeded, leading promoters to label this area as "El Daredo of the North." Hence, from 1896 until the Great Depression, gold business boomed in mountain towns like Ruby, Conconully, Barron, Nighthawk, Loup Loup, and Loomis.

The Methow shared in the wealth. The search started easy here, with stream panning and placer operations, but soon got down to hard-rock drilling and blasting.

Chinese placer miners were among the earliest to try their luck along the lower Methow and Columbia Rivers in 1860. The "China Ditch," built from three miles upstream on the Methow River to today's Pateros, trapped modest amounts of gold. Chinese placer miners worked the deposits of sand and gravel that contained particles of gold or other valuable heavy minerals. Gold is the most important mineral found in placer mining.

The rush up the valley may have begun in 1886 when word got out that Captain Joe White, a Methow Indian, discovered a big gold ledge on War Creek up the Twisp River.

Squaw Creek and the Red Shirt Mine hosted the first lower-valley booms. The town of Gilbert, up Twisp River Valley, served a slew of miners during the 1890s. A bit later, the Alder Mine sprang up just south of Twisp and continued sporadic production until the 1950s, turning out a million dollars worth of metals in its lifetime.

Extracting gold from the Methow's Rocky Mountains was never easy. Miners seeking riches from the Slate Creek area high in the rugged North Cascades faced formidable challenges. The rugged terrain of the region made access difficult and hauling freight dangerous. In an average winter, heavy snowfalls caused slides that poured down canyons. In some cases, buildings were demolished and miners buried alive. This district was first discovered by west side prospectors working up the Skagit River; however, because that route was so daunting, most elected to use the Methow access route.

Alex Barron arrived there first in 1893, discovering a "glory hole," which spawned a roaring boomtown bearing his name, near the Cascade Summit. Supplying this hungry camp proved a boom for both the town of Winthrop and founder Guy Waring's trading company. Two years later, Colonel Thomas Hart bought an interest in Slate Creek mines and began building a narrow-gauge (26 inches wide at one point) road into that district. Results of his hazardous project remain today as Hart's Pass—at 6,200 feet the highest roadway in Washington State. Infamous Dead Horse Point along the way marks the spot where an entire pack string of horses plunged off a cliff. Brothers Charles and Hazard Ballard took over Hart's task. They widened the road slightly, and eventually became involved with the Mammoth and Azurite mines, which continued operating through the 1930s.

Guy Waring, on right, and Alex Barron. (Photo from Okanogan County Historical Society collection).

Today, nothing but some tailings and a few decayed buildings survive where once feverish mining activity flourished. Thousands of claims remain, from Pateros to Hart's Pass, but almost none are being worked. "No one really got rich from mining here, but the glitter of gold is what first brought folks to Northeastern Washington." The gold fever subsided here just as it was breaking out elsewhere. In 1897-98, the stampeders headed for the Klondike and into the Caribou mining district of British Columbia. At one point, the town of Barron nearly emptied overnight. Alex Barron himself headed north.

Interested in learning more about historic Northeastern Washington's history? Then come step back in time with *Boom Towns & Relic Hunters of Northeastern Washington State* at **www.GhostTownsUSA.com** and enjoy your Wild West ghost town adventure.

Jerry Smith
Winthrop, Washington

Washington state map showing the six historic counties of Northeastern Washington: Okanogan, Chelan, Ferry, Kittitas, Pend Oreille, and Stevens.

Map of the United States showing the location of Washington state.

Ghost Towns of Northeastern Washington By County

A rare territorial check from Northeastern Washington dated May 31, 1888, signed on reverse side by Treasurer E.C. Sherman with a vignette of miners at the left.

GHOST TOWNS OF OKANOGAN COUNTY

In 1886, the north half of the Colville Indian Reservation was thrown open for mineral entry, and within weeks, hundreds of prospectors flooded in and staked hundreds of claims.

This was the area that would become known as Okanogan County—the mountains, valleys, and foothills of Moses, Tonasket, Joseph, and Sar-sarp-kin, famous Indian chiefs from another frontier. Men of the early West made a name for themselves in Okanogan County, men like "Okanogan" Smith, Guy Waring, Colonel Tom Hart, Chee Saw, and many others. It's the largest and one of the most fascinating counties in the state of Washington.

Okanogan is a Salish Indian word meaning "Rendezvous." Sometimes called "The Late Frontier," the Okanogan Valley saw habitation by Native Americans for thousands of years before a succession of explorers, prospectors, miners, trappers, cattlemen, settlers, loggers, farmers, missionaries, and orchardists arrived, providing in every respect a colorful history that is carried forward to the present day.

Here, a person only has to use his or her imagination and to wander long-forgotten ghost towns and abandoned town sites with colorful names like Ruby, Bodie, Loup Loup,

Photo on the left: Chief Moses on war pony. (Northwest Museum of Arts & Culture/Eastern Washington State Historical Society, Spokane, Washington). Photo on the right: Chief Joseph in ceremonial dress poses on painted horse in 1903. Before he posed for this picture, he exacted $10 from the artist. (MSCUA, University of Washington Libraries, NA1285).

Completely abandoned today, Bodie still stands as a classic ghost town mining camp.

Nighthawk and Silver just to mention a few. There's much to hold the history buff's attention: legends of hidden gold and long-lost million-dollar mines, several of which are still searched for by treasure hunters today. Others are intrigued by the age-old quest for gold. Several of these historic boomtowns of yesteryear still stand today, places like Nighthawk, Loomis, Old Molson, Chesaw, and Riverside—silent monuments to the past that have changed little in over 100 years.

We invite you to step back in time on a Wild West ghost town adventure and experience for yourself the history of Northeastern Washington. It's an experience you won't soon forget.

AENEAS: Community established around 1908. Location: 21 miles southwest of Republic on the west fork of the San Poil River. Center Sec. 8, T35N, and R31E.

Aeneas Valley is named for an Okanogan Indian chief who settled here in 1863 with his family and livestock, forsaking his ancestral lands and tribal role in the forested region west of the Okanogan River. Aeneas could not control the young men under him who wanted to kill invading white miners and settlers, yet he knew their course was futile. Chief Aeneas lived on his ranch until his death in about 1905.

ALMA: Community established around 1888. Location: SW/NE Sec. 17, T33N, and R26E. Town platted August 20, 1904. Was originally located on the site of present day Okanogan. It was renamed Pogue on September 16, 1905.

Frank J. Cummings a local merchant and ferryman, also known as "Pard" because he addressed everyone as "Pard." In 1891, during an Indian scare, a local defensive organization passed a resolution urging Cummings not to sell ammunition to the Indians.

ANGLIN: Community established around 1902. Location: On Bonaparte Creek, eight and one-half miles southeast of Tonasket NW/NE Sec. 2 T36N, R28E, SW/SE Sec. 34, T37N, R28E. Perhaps no pioneer town has so completely disappeared in Okanogan County as did the once-thriving community of Anglin.

At first glance, there is hardly a sign of that once-busy town. Occasionally, one can see the various level places and stone foundations on the windswept flat where Anglin buildings once stood.

Tom Anglin, a hardy young pioneer with a vision, scouted several communities before coming to a decision. With a six-horse outfit, carrying his wife, a dog, a supply wagon, and all their worldly possessions, Tom headed east up Bonaparte Creek from Parry's trading post and up the long winding cobblestone and sand-hole grade. Today, we know this road as State Highway 30, which takes us to Republic. After traveling just eight miles up that grueling grade, Tom's horses had had it. So had Tom and his wife, Molly.

They hauled to a stop, put the nosebags on the hungry horses, and sat down to discuss the situation. "Why not drive our stakes here?" mused Tom. His wife agreed. Early-day stagecoaches and freighter wagons were spotted here, where the traveler just had to stop for rest, water, and food. Word quickly got around that the Anglins hoped to have a community around them, and one after another, new dreamers arrived. A restaurant, saloon, blacksmith shop, and livery stable were built soon after. Those are the four cornerstones upon which many a dream town built its foundation.

Naturally, the town became known as "Anglin." By 1904, the freighter stop had become a town, a large enough one, in fact, that they put on a long-remembered Fourth of July celebration. However, greener pastures lured families away one by one.

Today, people driving up that highway can see various level places in the sod and stone foundations where Anglin buildings once stood in addition to a small apple orchard and two or three trees, long ago gone wild. A tiny four-inch sign reads "Anglin established 1902," and not far from this sign, across the road and on top of the hill is the Anglin cemetery. Truly the work of men's hands fades quickly away and goes back to dust.

ANTOINE: Community established around 1908. Location: Six miles northeast of Tonasket SW/SW Sec. 32, T38N, and R28E.

BARRON: Community established around 1893. Location: West side of Hart's Pass, about three miles from the Cascade Summit.

Overnight, Barron became a western boomtown sprouting multiple saloons, stores, and assorted buildings to serve the 2,500 miners employed in the district.

Dance-hall girls kicked up their high heels doing the can-can at the Barron Hotel. Most workers sometimes used bad judgment with their money, and as a result, gambling was rampant.

Guy Waring, Methow Trading Post in the former mining camp of Barron, located deep in the rugged mountains of Hart's Pass. (MSCUA, University of Washington Libraries, UW2318).

These miners were mostly middle-aged men, and they enjoyed adult amusements while at Barron, far from the constraints of the law and "proper" ladies. During its short, hectic lifetime in the Slate Creek District, the town of Barron had long-reaching effects. In 1907, however, when the mines in the area failed to produce promised riches, the inhabitants of Barron became panic-stricken, and within weeks, everyone deserted the town.

BECK: Community established around 1906. Location: On Loup Loup Creek, about 11 miles by road west of Okanogan and about nine miles northeast of Malott NE/SE Sec. 17, T33N, R25E.

BODIE: Community established around 1898. Location: On Toroda Creek four miles north of Old Toroda and 15 miles northeast of Wauconda SW Sec. 3, T38N, R31E.

In 1888, Henry Dewitz, attracted by the mineralized outcrops in the region, soon established a log building settlement at the mouth of Bodie Creek. By 1896, Bodie was firmly established with the usual restaurant, general store, smithy shop, livery barn, and several log cabins. Henry Dewitz struck the big lode barely a mile north of Bodie.

The pocket of ore purportedly yielded an amazing $80,000 in gold. The Dewitz brothers sold the mine to the Wrigley Brothers. The Wrigleys built a reduction mill in 1902. The mine began to make a name for itself and was called the Bodie Mine.

By 1917, however, the sporadic nature of the ore and a slow decline in values forced the Bodie Mine to close. For 17 more years, Bodie lay abandoned. Then, an increase in the price of gold triggered activity in the Bodie Mine once again.

This abandoned building was once the saloon/schoolhouse, and it still remains today in the historic ghost town mining camp of Bodie.

Finally, in 1944, after producing an estimated $1,250,000 in gold, the Bodie Mine shut down for good. Since then, the mill has fallen into decay, but the town site completely abandoned, still stands today as a classic ghost town.

BOLSTER: Community established around 1898. Location: Two miles north of Chesaw on Meyers Creek, two miles from the Canadian line NW/SE Sec. 9, T40N, R30E.

The early-day boomtown of Bolster was located within sight of the Canadian border. Bolster started in a mining flurry when the area was opened to mineral entry in 1896. Bolster was platted in 1899 by J.W. McBride. There were three stores, a post office, assay office (an assay is an analysis of an ore or metal to determine the proportion or purity of its ingredients), newspaper called *The Bolster Drill*, several saloons, Doctor Beale's office, and a three-story hotel. The boom collapsed in 1900.

By 1904, Bolster was practically deserted, but the post office remained until 1909. Today, it would be hard to tell as one drives by the old Bolster site that there had ever been a population of 200 or 300 souls. As you drive toward the Canadian boundary two miles north of Chesaw, three old, weather-beaten buildings can be seen standing in a field near the Pickering modern farm home. A casual visitor to this peaceful, quiet area might mistake them for abandoned homesteaders' shacks, little suspecting that they mark the Main Street where the gay, bustling town of Bolster once stood. In 1900, miners' picks and drills were active on both sides of this Myers Creek Valley, eventually stirring up considerable excitement at such properties as the nearby Gray Eagle and Tico mines.

The fact that Bolster had a newspaper gave it promise of becoming a large town. The history of early-day newspapers of the upper country is that of the pioneer printers and publishers—the courageous ones who came when there was little to live on, but much to live for. When trail-blazing town-builders platted a parcel of ground, drove their stakes, posted a sign, and said, "This is where the town will be," the very first man to put in an appearance was a printer. Arriving with a gunnysack full of type and a battered-up press or two, he took out his jack knife, sharpened a wooden pencil stud, hacked off a chaw of "Old Horseshoe," and he was in business! A newspaper was born.

The Bolster Drill died in its infancy, as did many other newspapers of the day. Morally and financially backed by John McBride, mine and town site promoter, *The Bolster Drill* was edited by Dan Jenkins. Dan was the son of W.D. Jenkins, then Washington's Secretary of State. The elder Jenkins was also connected with both the *Reveille* and the *Herald*, published in Bellingham, Washington. However, there was nothing to support a paper at Bolster, and its demise was inevitable. The plant reverted to McBride, godfather of Bolster. Later, much of *The Bolster Drill's* equipment was bought by Fred Fine and used in starting the *Oroville Gazette*.

Bolster boasted of a Board of Trade and also the Bolster Improvement Company. An advertisement of the latter institution stated: "Bolster has made a growth since October 1899 that no other town in Washington can show. From an Indian village of two log huts, in less than one year's time, over 90 substantial buildings now adorn the flat." By 1900, Chesaw and Molson had been started, and a town at Kipling had been planned. With the demise of *The Bolster Drill*, publication of the *Myers Creek News* at Chesaw began in February 1902.

BONAPARTE: Community established around 1903. Location: About 17 miles northeast of Tonasket, three miles west of Havillah, on Antoine Creek NW/ NE Sec. 2, T38N, R28E. Bonaparte was established when the U.S. government built a flour mill, shingle mill, and water-powered sawmill for the Indians in 1886. These mills were put in at the request of Chief Tonasket to help the Indians with some of the necessities of life. Around 1900, John Hone took a farm nearby and built a general merchandise store complete with living quarters. A post office was established here in 1903, but on January 15, 1908, the mail was discontinued, and the mail went to Havillah.

This ended Bonaparte's history as a town. The mills, which had been shut down in 1902, were soon dismantled. Some evidence still remains at the bottom of Fancher Dam covered with mud and debris. Today, the site of Bonaparte is flooded by Fancher Dam, which was built in 1926. Unlike many of Okanogan County's early-day boomtowns that faded away, Bonaparte will always have Bonaparte Mountain to carry on its name.

BREWSTER: Community established around 1903. Location: On Great Northern Railway, seven miles northeast of Pateros, 15 miles southwest of Malott on the west shore of the Columbia River, five miles below the mouth of the Okanogan River NE Sec.14, T30N, R24E. The original name for this site was Rich Bar, which was bestowed in 1862 when a gold discovery was made nearby. The report is that there were as many as 500 miners working the gravel along the river in the 15-mile span between present-day Pateros and Bridgeport. However, it was only a flurry, and the name Rich Bar was snuffed out with the rapid exit of the miners.

As settlers began to enter the Okanogan country in greater numbers, there grew a need for navigation up the Columbia River. The confluence of the Okanogan and Columbia Rivers was the limit to which steamers could go on the big river. About a mile above Virginia City, a man named John Bruster homesteaded a piece of land where there was an unusually smooth flat area on a cove where the water was deep enough to anchor a sternwheeler. Bruster sold this portion of his land to the manager of the Steamboat Company. On it was platted Bruster's town on April 10, 1896. Gradually, all that was Virginia City moved to Bruster along with all of the store buildings except the post office. The Post Office Department would not accept the name Bruster, so the name Brewster was submitted and accepted.

CARLTON: Community established around 1907. Location: In the Methow Valley 12 miles northwest of the town of Methow. SW/NE Sec. 29, T32N, R22E. In 1903, William J. Fleming arranged for the moving of a two-story store, hotel, and two houses to the mouth of Texas Creek. As Carlton was taking shape, Carl Dillards purchased "Locust Lodge" from the Sumpter family. One afternoon in 1907, a group of ladies who were visiting in the Dillard home discussed a name for the new town. Among the guests were Mrs. Joseph Liebl and her mother, Mrs. McConnell. Out of respect to their host, Mrs. McConnell suggested it be called "Carl's Town." After some discussion, the ladies decided on "Carlton."

The Carlton Hotel still remains at the old Carlton town site.

People came by steamboat up the Columbia River to Ives Landing between 1896 and 1900, at which time Central Ferry's Landing was changed to Pateros. Others came by train, horseback, or stagecoach. Many pioneers followed established trails into the Methow Valley. Platted on August 23, 1907, Carlton's location was specified as SW/NE Sec. 29, T32N, and R22E. This was just across the road from where the old Carlton Hotel still stands today. By 1927, it was learned where new highway No. 12 would be built and where the new bridge would cross the Methow River. Since the highway would be a quarter of a mile from the original town of Carlton, they decided to move the buildings close so that the new highway would go right pass their front doors.

The earliest school in Carlton was built in 1907. A brick school, which was built in the early 1920s, still stands today, and is a private residence. Locust trees, planted when Carlton was a new town, can still be seen along the property. Locust Lodge was named for them. Farming has slowed down in the Methow Valley, however, there are always new additions to the town. There is a motel with a swimming pool and a small grocery store that sells the much-sought-after Carlton fly. Everyone is friendly, so be sure to stop by when you are in the Methow Valley and say howdy!

CHAPAKA: Community established around 1895. Location: 13 miles north of Loomis, 35 miles west of Oroville about one-half mile west of Similkameen River.

CHESAW: Community established around 1898. Location: 11 miles southeast of Molson SW Sec. 21, NW Sec. 28, T40N, and R30E. In an almost forgotten corner of the Okanogan County remains what is left of the once-historic town of Chesaw. In the early days, this town was on the edge of greatness in the mining world.

The name of the town is unusual. Placer gold was discovered in the area before the turn of the century. The result was a stampede of miners. When the miners arrived, to their surprise they discovered numbers of Oriental miners already in the area. One of the most prominent of the Orientals was a former placer miner called Chee Saw. He had a small ranch and store not too far from the diggings. The white

Chesaw's boom town days included two hotels, a large three-story livery barn, a blacksmith shop, two department stores, one hardware store, a barber shop, post office, an assay office, three saloons, a bank, and three grocery stores.

miners soon began purchasing their supplies from the Chinese merchant. Before long, the phrase "Chee Saw's" became a byword for fair prices and honest deals, and eventually it evolved into simply "Chesaw," the name the town bears today.

By the turn of the century, the region had become a lodestone for hard-rock miners, and fantastic discoveries were made. Chesaw quickly developed into a substantial mining town. By 1910 there were 40 buildings. Those were the days when Chesaw was on the rise and the sounds familiar to a mining boomtown could be heard: the curses and shouts of the miners, the click of poker chips in the saloons where a mine was bought or sold on a handshake deal, and the noises of the town as new buildings appeared almost daily.

Those years were short-lived, however. The assays simply didn't carry their values, and one by one, most of the mines were abandoned. Chesaw, like so many other hard luck-mining towns, declined. As the years have passed, the buildings lining Main Street have slowly disappeared. The abandoned ranches and deserted mines are a reminder of those days when gold was king in the Okanogan Highlands.

CHANCELLOR: Community established around 1872. Location: Slate Creek area, Hart's Pass, and Methow Valley. Nestled on the side of Slate Creek, this remnant of a small town remains fairly quiet, detached from civilization and forgotten by the Methow Valley even though Chancellor was one of the first and more prominent mining towns in the area. Prospectors came to the area in 1872 amid a rush for gold. Mines popped up at Three Fools Peak, Barron, and other potential veins all over the upper Methow region. For years, prospectors staked their claims in Chancellor. Some hit a small jackpot, but many left empty-handed. By 1892, the town was practically abandoned. Some rotting structures still remain.

One of many deserted old log structures that still remain in the rugged Hart's Pass area.

CIRCLE CITY: Community established around 1907. Location: Halfway between Oroville and Molson on Nine Mile Road. Circle City derived its name from

Circle City derived its name from the nearby loop the railroad track made as it wound its way up the grade from an elevation of 920 feet at Oroville to 3,700 feet at Molson. It was 28 miles long, nearly twice that of the wagon road. (Photo from Okanogan County Historical Society collection).

the nearby loop the railroad track as it wound its way up the grade from the elevation of 920 feet to 3,700 feet. It was 28 miles long, nearly twice that of the wagon road.

Circle had a section house, an unsuccessful water tank, depot with a few grocery items, and a school. In 1907, with an average of two and one-half percent grade, the railroad line was completed. Here, westbound trains had to stop to cool their brakes. The school was organized in 1907, and the new schoolhouse was built in 1912. Due to many boomtowns dying out and becoming ghost towns, and the coming of trucks, the railroad was pulled out in 1932. Although Circle City never was a city or even really a town, it certainly played a role in the history of yesteryear.

The old Loop railroad bed can still be seen today in various places where the loco-motive once ran.

In 1931, the railroad was abandoned between Molson and Oroville. The tracks were pulled in 1932. These relics from the past are near the ghost town site of Circle City, a testament to those railroad boom days gone by.

CLOVER: Community established around 1892. Location: On Salmon Creek, three and one-half miles northeast of Okanogan NE Sec. 36, T34N, R25E. Not much ever existed here. Clover, like other places, never consisted of much more then a post office. Established May 24, 1892, it served the Ruby area after that post office closed. Mail was supplied by the Malott-Conconully Star Route. However, the Clover post office was too near Okanogan to survive. The office was discontinued on March 30, 1901, and the mail went to Conconully.

CONCONULLY: Community established around 1888. Location: 15 miles northwest of Omak, on Salmon Creek SW Sec. 6, T35N, and R25E. The settlement was first called "Salmon City."

At first glance, you would probably never suspect that this small town in the hills of western Okanogan was once the county seat. It was a beacon for prospectors all over the west. They came streaming in, first to Ruby, an overnight mining camp just south of Conconully.

It originally was known as "Salmon City" after mineralized ledges of high-grade ore was discovered in the Salmon Creek area in 1886. Before long, Salmon City was born. Certainly, Salmon City was more suited to be the county seat then its smaller rival of Ruby, and its citizens began working toward that goal. Ruby was located in a narrow canyon and lacked good access by road, whereas Salmon City was more favorably located. The area around Salmon City had open grasslands, Salmon Creek, meadows, and Conconully Lake. This area was more pleasant, refined, and lawful.

By 1891, the name of the town had been changed to Conconully, and it had become the county seat. It is believed the Indians called this entire area, including the lake, "Conconully," and in Indian means "the beautiful land on the bunch grass flats."

For several years, Conconully flourished. The silver was flowing in steadily, and Main Street became quite a showplace. In 1893, the price of silver dropped, but even that failed to halt its progress. In 1894, a wall of water from Salmon Creek swept down Main Street, destroying many of the businesses in its path. The town never quite recovered, and gradually, Conconully began to fade. Finally when the county

It is believed the Indians called this entire area, including the lake, "Conconully," which means "The beautiful land of the bunch grass flats."

seat was lost to the town of Okanogan in 1914, a gloom settled over the once boom-town. By the 1920s, much of the splendor of Conconully had vanished.

The town is still there today, nestled in the hills. Not much remains from the 1890s, but many abandoned mines throughout the area attest to the fact that Conconully was the most important town in the Okanogan County in its day.

COULEE DAM: Community established around 1934. Location: On the north Columbia riverbank beside Grand Coulee Dam. NW Sec. 6, T28N, R31E.

DISAUTEL: Community established around 1919. Location: 15 miles southeast of Omak, center Sec. 13, T33N, and R28E. Two miles west of Disautel. Biles-Coleman logging camps were opened and closed as needed. The largest was Camp 6. There, 100 men were "falling 6,000 acres of forest a year," and a train left each afternoon with 19 cars of logs. In 1929, Biles-Coleman moved its headquarters to Disautel.

This logging village soon had a population of 276, homes for 40 families, a school with two teachers, and two stores. Disautel was a bustling community until the late 1930s when improvements to the Nespelem Highway enabled most workers in the logging community to commute from Omak. In the early 1930s, the mills started shutting down as the Great Depression spread across the nation.

ELMER CITY: Community established around 1939. Location: Three miles north of Coulee Dam Village, on the east shore of the Columbia River W/NW/SW Sec. 20, T29N, R31E. Two miles downstream from Mason City, Elmertown (later Elmer City) was platted on March 2, 1937, on a portion of what had been Elmer Seaton's homestead. Elmer Seaton operated a ferry here for several years. The town grew as an overflow of the Coulee Dam construction town of Mason City.

EPLEY: Community established around 1906. Location: On Pogue Flat, two miles northwest of Omak NW Sec. 27, T34N, R26E. Epley consisted of not much more then a post office, which was established on March 20, 1906. It was situated on what is known as Pogue Flat at a point about two miles northwest of present-day Omak on the road from Omak to Conconully. At this time, settlers were beginning to take up homesteads on the flat, and a post office here served to direct travelers over the flat rather then along the old river road. Mail came daily by stage, running from Riverside to Alma. On May 31, 1914, mail was discontinued here and went to Omak.

GILBERT: Community established around 1909. Location: Twisp River Valley near North Creek and the Twisp River. In the Twisp River Valley, the town of Gilbert grew up in the mid-1890s as mining development in the area went into high gear. Gilbert (the mining camp) consisted of a half dozen buildings. Most miners only lived there in the summer since no services were available, except possibly a black-smith shop.

Gilbert was probably used as a jumping-off point for the many prospectors in the region who were constantly scouring the area close by in their never-ending search for

*Cody and Lloyd Smith at the historic ghost town mining camp of Gilbert
where this 1895 vintage Gilbert miner's cabin remains today.*

bonanza ore. Two old mining cabins still stand in Gilbert today. Some stone foundations and depressions in the ground identify where additional structures once stood.

GOLD HILL: Camp founded around 1880. Location: On Gold Hill six miles
due west of Loomis. Gold Hill in Okanogan County was never a platted town, but
rather was a gold camp for many miners and prospectors in this general area. There's
not much that remains of this once-booming camp from yesteryear. What does
remain, however, are four small log cabins and a rather large bunk/cookhouse.

The remains of Gold Hill mining camp, bunkhouse, and cookhouse.

The cookhouse for the most part has given up to Mother Nature and is caving
in on itself. The log cabins are still standing, but only one remains with the roof
intact. Another one built next to a gully and standing about four feet high has a
unique rock foundation.

The camp itself was founded about 1880 and was out of business around 1893,
when the silver crash happened in that same year and forced most mines to shut
down production.

One of the few remaining buildings at the ghost town camp of Gold Hill.

There were many mines in the area, and all produced gold and silver right up to the present day. Mule trains took all the supplies into camp, and there was no formal road until around 1930. The present-day road into Gold Hill is not in good shape and is steep—four-wheel drive is needed to get there. The main mine that supported the camp flooded with water and is no longer accessible. There are several other short tunnels in the area that still carry gold to a certain extent. Gold Hill is an intriguing mountain, and it's no wonder the old timers decided to work it. The site of Gold Hill and the surrounding mines in the area are on private property. Mines and mine shafts are DANGEROUS. Please respect "No Trespassing" signs—the owner puts them there for a reason.

GOLDEN: Community established around 1889. Location: Six miles southwest of Oroville on the northwest corner of Wannacut Lake, SE/NE Sec. 11, T39N, R26E. It would be difficult to imagine where the town of Golden once stood, although it was quite the mining town in its day. In 1887, prospectors discovered some outcrops of oxidized quarts to the west of Wannacut Lake that was laced with "free gold." It was a bonanza find, and almost overnight a stampede of hundreds of prospectors streamed into the region.

On the strength of these findings, a mining town sprang to life, and by 1892, more then 30 buildings stood on the flat between the mines and Wannacut Lake. The area held high hopes then, so it was only fitting that the mining town be called "Golden."

HASSAN: Community established around 1910. Location: Sprang up in the Pine Creek area about 15 miles southwest of Tonasket. SW Sec. 25, T37N, R25E.

HAVILLAH: Community established around 1905. Location: 20 miles southeast of Oroville near the head of Antoine Creek SW Sec. 32, T39N, and R29E. Nestled in the foothills on the north side of Bonaparte Mountain, Havillah was settled quickly when homesteaders spread across what had been the Moses Reservation. In 1900, the north half of the Colville Reservation was opened to settlement; in

1916, the south half was. First, there were mostly Methodists in the area, but soon it became a German-Lutheran farming community. Martin Schweikert rode into Havillah country early in 1904.

He soon took up a homestead and set up a grist mill, and in a short while, a flour mill and store in 1905. That same year, the government approved the name Havillah, and a post office was established on September 29, 1905. The post office was discontinued on March 31, 1944, and the mail went to Tonasket. The first church was constructed in 1905. By 1906, a two-story, four-room parsonage was completed. Havillah has not seen the change that some earlier-day boomtowns have experienced, but it's still one of the most beautiful areas to be found in this county, especially with its nostalgic old-style church setting and flour-mill school house, which has been restored.

IVES: Community established around 1896. Location: On the Columbia River at the northeast edge of present-day Pateros NE Sec. 36, T30N, R23E. This was also called "Ives Landing" and "Central Ferry." The founder of what later became Pateros, Lee Ives, had driven a herd of horses from Kittitas Valley and begun farming near the mouth of the Methow River.

In 1894-95, Ives built his landmark hotel on the banks of the Columbia River. When the spring runoff of 1894 flooded the dinning room, Ives and his wife Rena served meals from a tent. This community became known as Ives Landing. Its first post office in 1895 was named Nera, which may have been Rena (Mrs. Ives) with a couple of letters transposed. This name was soon changed to Ives.

KARTAR: Community established around 1922. Location: About 32 miles northwest of Grand Coulee Village, about nine miles south of Omak Lake SW Sec. 34, T31N, R28E.

KIPLING: Community established around 1901. Location: About nine miles southwest of Chesaw on Tonasket Creek NW/NE Sec. 5, T39N, and R29E. Two years before the north half of the Colville Indian Reservation opened for homesteading, a trading post was established on the beaten path of Rock Creek, B.C. Canada. It was known as the Hawthorne Store.

In October 1900, 95 homesteaders came here to file on their homestcads. Those filings were rushed daily by horseback to Waterville. G.H. Tamblin was the surveyor and homestead locator, assisted by Fred Warren; Tamblin was also the founder of Kipling. On October 1, 1900, the Kipling town site was surveyed and Kipling Mercantile was established. A post office was established on August 5, 1901. There was also the "Halfway House" that was located near the Shaw residence. Shaw was one of the postmasters.

The "Halfway House" was a place freighters and horses rested and repairs were made. A schoolhouse was built in 1902 near the Kipling Mercantile. Then, in 1942, Kipling School joined with Molson. Doctor Beale filed on the town site for his homestead and was the surrounding county's doctor for many years.

The little community of Kipling faded away soon after Molson started growing. If you could locate a rare old map, you may be able to find the town of Kipling on it.

Farming, cattle raising, and timber are still the sources of income for remaining Kipling area residents.

KNOB HILL: Community established around the early 1900s. Location: About 10 miles southwest of Chesaw. Homesteaders settled the area during the early 1900s. There were still wild horses from the Indian days roaming the country then. By 1908, the Knob Hill folks felt there was enough of a population that a better mail service was due them. They were granted a rural route out of Chesaw.

The schoolhouse was located by the Bake Lakes, a short distance from where the Knob Hill Grange Hall was built. The area never had a town or post office. A water-powered sawmill was built on nearby Myers Creek in 1904. Its water wheel was 35 feet in diameter and four feet wide. Times have changed, but Knob Hill remains today.

LOOMIS: Community established around 1891. Location: 16 miles northwest of Tonasket on Sinlahekin Creek Center Sec. 1, T38N, and R25E. Originally called "Loomistown" and "Loomiston." It was one of the great mining towns in Okanogan County at one time. One of the first settlers was the pioneer merchant, Julius Allen Loomis, who built the first store on the site and called the place "Loomiston."

In 1886, the Colville Indian Reservation was thrown open and hundreds of prospectors flooded in. By 1891, the influx had turned Loomis into a boomtown. Its three-block long Main Street was lined with buildings, including a total of eight saloons and two dance halls.

In 1893, the bottom suddenly dropped out of the silver market and threw Loomis into a tailspin. It stayed that way until 1898, when interest in mining suddenly revived. Loomis roared back to life. By 1899, its population was well over 500. Loomis was a tough mining town in its days, typical of many mining camps scattered throughout Okanogan County.

However, the price of silver dropped again. After that, Loomis declined rapidly and the miners drifted away. Today, the Loomis of old has all but vanished. The colorful Main Street is no more, although a few buildings from the past still survive.

Photo on the left: Main Street in Loomis, Okanogan County, circa 1908. (Photo from Okanogan County Historical Society collection). Photo on the right: A view down Main Street Loomis. Today, the gold rush days and buildings of Loomistown have vanished forever.

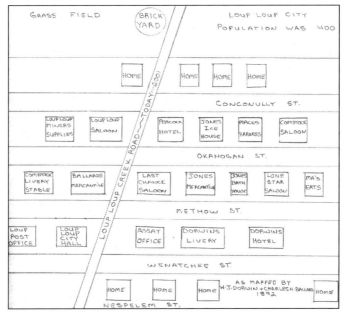

Loup Loup City as mapped by W.J. Dorwin and Charles H. Ballard in 1892.

LOUP LOUP: Community established around 1888. Location: Eight miles south of Conconully SE/SE/NW Sec.31, T35N, and R25E. On August 14, 1888, Loup Loup was the first town in Okanogan County to be platted. About eight miles south and slightly west of Conconully is the deserted town site of Loup Loup, which was once the scene of more mining activity than any other spot in Okanogan County.

Millionaires were produced there in minutes. Loup Loup, which lies only a couple of miles over Ruby Ridge and west of the Ruby town site, was a flourishing town in its day. This once-bustling mining settlement had 18 businesses and several streets.

There are no known pictures of the town, but Loup Loup had two hotels, four saloons, an ice house, two mercantile stores, an assay station, livery stable, city hall, post office, bath house, harness shop, miners' supplies, and Ma's Eats. Depreciation in silver in 1893 marked the immediate downfall of the town. The one large company operating there quit, the miners left, and the lights were rapidly extinguished in this one-time boomtown.

Today, no traces remain of this once-million-dollar town.

Businesses in Loup Loup City

The following is a partial list of businesses that were in Loup Loup at one time or another:

Loup Loup Miners Supplies	Jones Ice House	Loup Loup City Hall
Loup Loup Saloon	Macks Harness	Assay Office
Comstock Saloon	Livery Stable	Dorwins Hotel
Last Chance Saloon	Jones Bath House	Ballards Mercantile
Lone Star Saloon	Ma's Eats	Jones Mercantile
Peacock Hotel	Loup Loup Post Office	

MALOTT: Community established around 1890. Location: 15 miles northeast of Brewster, nine miles southwest of Okanogan, on the Okanogan River at mouth of Loup Loup Creek SW/SW Sec. 9, T32N, R25E. A meadow at the mouth of Loup Loup Creek nine miles southwest of Okanogan had been inhabited by whites since 1886. That's when Leonard C. and Mary Malott settled there with the three Hedges brothers, George, Albert, and Ed, as neighbors. Almost from the start, the Malott place served as a stop-over point for travelers. The Malott's huge barn could shelter 28 horses.

As early as 1890, L.C. Malott had a post office in his home. A town did not take shape, however, until 1909, when the Helensdal Investment Co. of Seattle purchased land from the Malotts. Hedges and James C. Burdett laid out the town of Malott. In 1910, John and Annie Hilderbrand, Ruby and Chiliwhist pioneers, opened a hotel in Malott. Transients, drummers (traveling salesman), orchard developers, railroad workers, and others kept the hotel and additional establishments busy.

MAZAMA: Community established around 1900. Location: 14 miles northwest of Winthrop on the Methow River SE Sec. 25, T36N, and R19E. Mazama boomed as the departure point for mining towns in the rugged Hart's Pass area such as Barron, Chancellor, and Robinson. It remains little more then a crossroads today, with a store, gas station, and post office.

Guy Waring, a leading merchant and owner of the Methow Trading Company of Winthrop, suggested the name of Mazama. The place had been called "Goat Creek" by the residents for a creek that flowed southward around Goat Mountain. For some unexplained reason, the Post Office Department would not accept the names "Goat Creek" or "Goat Mountain." Mr. Waring explained that Mazama was the Greek word for mountain goat, and this name was accepted.

The first settlers in this area were squatters who afterwards became homesteaders.

METHOW: Community established around 1894. Location: On Methow River, nine miles northwest of Pateros NW Sec. 2, T30N, R22E. In 1889, W.A. Bolinger

Historic Bolinger homestead located on private property.

came to the little settlement of Squaw Creek, observed the frenzied activity, saw a need, and started a general store.

The Squaw Creek boom ended as fast as it had started, and Bolinger could see that the end was near. He moved his store three miles up the Methow River from the mouth of Squaw Creek to what is now today the town of Methow. The first house that Bolinger homesteaded in 1892 still stands there today. Later, he built a house entirely of granite rock. If you drive through the town of Methow, you can view this historical landmark, which is on private property.

MISSION: Established as St. Mary's Mission around 1889. Location: About seven miles southeast of Omak on Omak Creek Center Sec. 9, T33N, and R27E. Established as Omak on November 26, 1902. Etienne de Rogue renamed it to Mission on April 3, 1907.

Father Etienne de Rogue was a French Jesuit who had charge of the St. Mary's Mission, which he founded in 1889. Chief Joseph and Chief Moses attended services here, and the priest fluently spoke the Salish tongue in his work with the Indians. The name of the mission was St. Mary's from the start, but the priest chose Omak when naming the post office, perhaps because the Indians referred to it as such. When the present Omak settlement sought a post office, Father de Rogue was persuaded to change the name to Mission. The mission has suffered a series of fires over the years, but has continued to operate. A few of the original buildings remain today.

MOLSON: Community established around 1900. Location: 15 miles northeast of Oroville Center Sec. 8, T40N, and R29E. Some past ghost towns just refuse to give up the ghosts. The once boomtown of Molson was started in 1900 by George B. Meacham, promoter, and John W. Molson, investor. Molson operated the largest brewing company in Canada and owned the Molson Bank with branches in every province in Canada.

Built in 1900 at a cost of $8,500, it was one of the finest hotels in Okanogan County. The 34 rooms were nearly always filled. The rates were from 50 cents to $1.00, and meals were 35 cents. Tonasket Hotel was destroyed by fire in June 1924. (Photo from Okanogan County Historical Society collection).

Soon, many mining claims were staked and the town site was platted. Before long, the town's population reached 300. Buildings could not be built fast enough, and many had to live in tents. Soon there was a newspaper, three general stores, an attorney, a doctor and drug store, three saloons, a dance hall, livery barn, blacksmith shop, assay office, and a three-story hotel complete with a two-story outhouse. It was called Hotel Tonasket, named after the great Okanogan Indian chief.

After Molson's first boom busted, the Molson Company withdrew its backing and the population dwindled fast. In June 1901, there were only 13 people living in Molson. By 1903, though homesteaders were moving in, there was little difference in the town. It served as a stopping-off place for settlers moving into the area.

Early in 1905, with the news that the route of the railroad was definitely coming through Molson, things started booming again. In the meantime, J.H. McDonald filed on 160 acres for a homestead—that 160 acres also included 40 acres that the Molson Town Site Company was developing into the town of Old Molson. The Tonasket Hotel and other buildings were already on this land.

Classic old Wild West town of Old Molson.

On April 15, 1909, McDonald published a notice for "all persons living or residing or doing business on said tract of land or any part thereof to depart forewith from said land and to stay off." When it became evident that clear titles could not be obtained, a New Molson was platted near the railroad tracks. Disgusted citizens founded New Molson a half-mile north. People, businesses, post office, everything moved to the New Molson site. Its railroad station, elevation 3,708 feet, was the highest in Washington State. New Molson mushroomed, but the glory was short-lived, as the depression took its toll. The railroad was taken out in mid 1930s, and New Molson became a quiet agricultural community.

Old Molson faded away, but the memories of those old glory days still linger on in those old weathered, worn buildings, where the ghosts refuse to surrender. Today, the three old town sites of the boomtown days still remain: New Molson, Old Molson, and Central Molson.

Photo on the left: The Poland China Mine assay office was moved from that historic mine site north of Old Molson to the Old Molson museum historical grounds. Photo on the right: The original Molson State Bank building remains today at the Old Molson outdoor museum ghost town site.

The Molson red brick school museum in the fifties had an average daily attendance of 110 to 120 pupils. Today, visitors can tour the museum and enjoy the many exhibits and splendor from the boomtown days. About two blocks from the old school is another part of Old Molson Museum. This part of the museum is where the original boomtown of "Old Molson" once stood, with assay office, bank building, old homestead cabins, saloon, law office, machine shed with equipment, a few smaller structures, a windmill, and a great deal of other old relics. Volunteers from the Molson Historical Society will assist you with any questions you may have.

And oh yes, pardner, please don't leave until you've had a chance to sample one of the museum's fresh-baked homemade pastries with a hot cup of fresh brewed coffee. So folks, kick back awhile and enjoy the boomtown days of yesteryear in Old Molson.

MONSE: Community established around 1916. Location: On Okanogan River, seven miles northeast of Brewster, on the west side of the river and on the Great Northern Railway. Center Sec. 34, T31N, and R25E. Monse was a trading post in pioneer times, becoming in 1916 a flourishing supply center for south half-homesteaders. Initially called Lumsden after the prospector who operated it intermittently between trips to and from Spokane, this was the nearest place from which supplies could be bought. Lumsden made the road trip of 300 miles with four-horse team and wagon in 15 days or longer, depending upon the weather and conditions of the roads.

NESPELEM: Community established around 1899. Location: 34 miles southeast of Omak, 18 miles north of Grand Coulee, on Nespelem River SW Sec. 19, NW Sec. 30 T31N, R31E, SE Sec. 24. NE Sec. 25, T31N, R30E. Nespelem at one time was a subagency for the Colville Reservation. Nespelem is an Indian word meaning, "large meadow beside a stream." The first agency doctor, the zealous photographer

Photo on the left: The historic gravesite of Chief Joseph at Nespelem. Photo oabove: This rare and historic photo was taken in 1905 at Chief Joseph's burial at Nespelem. Tombstone inscription facing the camera reads: He led his people in the Nez Perce War of 1877. Died Sept. 21, 1904. (MSCUA, University of Washington Libraries, NA614).

Edward H. Latham, arrived at Nespelem in 1890. His charges included an effort to overcome the "superstitious rites and barbarous customs" of local medicine men.

In 1898, Congress, pressured by miners and without consulting any Indians whatsoever, opened the south half of the reservation to mineral entry. This produced a swarm of miners with ore wagons rumbling past Nespelem and steamboats loading concentrates at the mouth of Nespelem Creek. The subagency exploded into a boomtown. F.M. Daugherty opened its first store. However, of the 11,072 mining claims eventually posted on the south half, most were fraudulent, intended mainly to reserve land until such time as it could be legally occupied by whites for farming or grazing. Chief Joseph's and Chief Moses' sacred burial sites are located at Nespelem.

NIGHTHAWK: Community established around 1902. Location: On Great Northern Railway, 12 miles west of Oroville, 12 miles north of Loomis, on Similkameen

By 1903, there was a general store, Nighthawk Hotel, railroad station, saloon, and several other establishments, including a house of ill repute, shown here.

River NW Sec. 13, T40N, R25E. Nighthawk came into being when that country in the northwestern corner of Okanogan County was a beacon for prospectors. With Oroville to the east, Loomis to the southwest, and some spectacular mineral finds in between those two centers, it was not long before a stopping place called "Nighthawk" grew up around a ferry crossing just to the east of Miner's Bend in the heart of the mineral belt.

By 1903, there was a general store, railroad station, the Nighthawk Hotel, house of "ill repute," and saloon. Although the mining eventually subsided, Nighthawk survived, and down through the decades it has remained almost exactly as it was in the early 1900s. The prospectors and miners search no more through those barren but beautiful hills in the numbers they once did, but their legacy may still be seen.

Ore tailings of long-dead mines cascading down the mountainsides, abandoned and weathered buildings, and deserted workings mark the old location of Nighthawk, almost unchanged. This part of western Okanogan County abounds with old historic mines, decades of old buildings, trails, homesteads, landmarks, and a host of other fascinating reminders of the west of yesteryear.

The once-bustling Nighthawk Hotel built in 1903 stands today as an historic reminder of what once was.

NINE MILE: The Nine Mile community was located west of Molson on what is known today as Nine Mile Road. There were never any business establishments at Nine Mile, but the railroad tracks from Molson to Oroville went through this community.

There was a railway siding at Nine Mile where the train stopped for water from the tower and to cool its brakes. Here, loads of wheat and cords of firewood were picked up to take to market. The railroad was the main source of income for the school, the first one being located in a tent in 1906.

With several Indian allotments nearby, both whites and Indians attended this school. At one time there were 36 pupils with one teacher for all of the grades. A small frame house was built in 1908 and used as the second school, and a nice, larger school was built in 1913. The big school building burned in 1935, and school had to be held once again in the old second schoolhouse until 1938.

OKANOGAN: Community established originally as "Alma" about 1888 after Alma Kahlow, daughter of a Prussian farmer living here.. Location: Four miles southwest of Omak, on Great Northern Railway, nine miles northeast of Malott, at junction of Salmon Creek with the Okanogan River. NW Sec. 16, T33N, R26E.

The town of Okanogan began as a trading post established near the mouth of Salmon Creek by Frank "Pard" Cummings in 1886 when the Chief Moses Indian Reservation was thrown open to white settlement. The name changed to Okanogan, the Indian name for the river that flows through the valley, in 1907.

Okanogan Hotel, with the Bassett line stage about to depart for Brewster around 1907. (Photo from Okanogan County Historical Society collection.)

OKANOGAN CITY: Community established around 1860. Location: It was reportedly on the south side of the Similkameen River, somewhere between Nighthawk and Shanker's Bend. This old mining camp on the Similkameen River claimed a shifting population of more than 2,000 placer miners in 1860. The exact location of the original site of the camp has never been determined.

Somewhere along this stretch of the Similkameen River between Nighthawk and Shanker's Bend stood the haphazard collection of tents and shacks they called Okanogan City.

Like most temporary placer mining camps, it was primarily a tent town that lasted only a few hectic months. After the rush subsided, however, there were few permanent remains left to indicate where it had once stood. Although this historic placer camp was the greatest of all of the placer camps in early Washington history, the original site of Okanogan City has never been found. Undoubtedly, the site still lies somewhere along the south side of the river—truly a vanished camp from yesteryear.

OLEMA: Community established around 1896. Location: Seven and one-half miles west of Malott on Chiliwhist Creek NE Sec. 10, T32N, R24E. In 1890, there were only seven men and two women settlers at this town site. However, the population increased so substantially that by 1896 there was a demand for a post office. It was established on November 17, 1896. This country known as the Chiliwhist is a high, basin-like area surrounded by timbered mountains. It lies above and beyond the hills along the river where the creek of the same name empties into the Okanogan River. The name is of Indian origin, descriptive of the area, and is said to mean "big hole above a creek" and also "an opening above a waterfall or creek."

In Olema, like in most boomtowns, came the time when kerosene lights in the windows of the cabins in the Chiliwhist began to go out one by one. Dry years followed dry years, bringing discouragement and tax bills that could not be paid. Many 160-acre tracts went to the county for unpaid taxes. The few remaining settlers were those who were able to extend their acreage and still try to rough out a living.

OMAK: Community established around 1902. Location: On Great Northern Railway, four miles north of Okanogan on west bank of the Okanogan River S Sec. 26, NW Sec. 35, T34N, R26E. Omak was platted in 1907 and incorporated in 1911. It is Okanogan County's largest city. Omak was created when Dr. J. I. Pogue encouraged Ben Ross, who had purchased a homestead relinquishment four miles north of Okanogan, to plat another town. Ross was an Illinois surveyor and civil engineer. He was considering such a venture anyway and spent the fall of 1906 squinting down rows of pine stakes driven into an alfalfa field bordering the Okanogan River. In January 1907, Ross filed a 20-acre plat extending from present-day Bartlett Street south to First and from Douglas Street to the Okanogan River. At that time, the community consisted of an icehouse Ross filled from the Okanogan River if it froze each January. His 25-foot lots sold briskly, however, and within months there was an expanding business district. Omak is the home of the famous Omak Stampede and World-Famous Suicide Race, started in 1933 and 1935, respectively. The city's eastern portion lies within the Colville Indian Reservation.

OPHIR: Community established around 1890. Location: On Great Northern Railway, five miles south of Malott on the west side of the Okanogan River NW Sec. 5, T31N, R25E.

Ophir was about halfway between Brewster and Malott on the Old Stage Road—the first stop out of Brewster where the first horse changes were made. This site was on a bench about one half-mile from the Okanogan River and was the homestead of James B. Watson.

Ophir had a post office that was established on June 13, 1890. One old-timer described the town of Ophir as "never more then a ranch house of James B. Watson" in which was a store and post office serving the surrounding ranch settlers.

OROVILLE: Community established around 1893. Location: On Great Northern Railway, 16 miles north of Tonasket, four miles south of the Canadian line, at the southern end of Osoyoos Lake from which flows the Okanogan River. E Sec. 28, T40N, R27E.

In 1891, Robert Allison freighted in goods and supplies from Loomis to open a small store and eating establishment. His location was named "Oro"—Spanish for gold. The following spring, when James M. Hagerty published the first issue of *The Madre d'Oro*, Allison still had the only completed building in town. Allison had departed, but his fine building served as a store, restaurant, boarding house, and stage station. The rest of the town of Oro, including the newspaper, was housed in tents.

In 1893, a post office was crammed into the Allison building. The post office department added "ville" to "Oro" to avoid confusion with an existing post office, Oso, in Snohomish County. In time, Oroville began replacing tents with frame buildings. In 1906, a Great Northern Railway freight agent was dispatched to Okanogan County to size up potential revenues. This agent counted 17 saloons in Oroville, some of them hotel bars—far more than any other town in Okanogan County. The community flourished further when the railroad arrived from Molson in 1907.

PATEROS: Community established around 1895. Location: On Great Northern Railway, 19 miles northeast of Chelan, 30 miles southwest of Okanogan, at junction of Methow and Columbia rivers. SW Sec. 36, T30N, R23E. Ives Landing, which later became known as Pateros, was established around 1896 by its founder, Lee Ives. Having driven a herd of his horses from Kittitas Valley, he began farming near the mouth of the Methow River in company with 50 teepees of Indians and about 20 Chinese miners still placer mining from the Chinese Ditch.

In 1894-95, Ives built his landmark hotel on the banks of the Columbia River. Its first post office was established in 1895. In 1900, Charles E. Nosler, a Spanish-American War veteran, acquired most of the town site. He renamed it Pateros after a village built largely on stilts he had known in the Philippines. Three years later, Pateros had grown to four commercial establishments and nine residences. Nosler sold the site to J.C. Steiner, who promoted the area so vigorously that for a time Pateros ranked as the principal rail-shipping point between Wenatchee and Oroville.

PONTIAC RIDGE: Community established around 1903-1904. Location: Southwest of Chesaw on Pontiac Ridge. The Pontiac Ridge area begins several miles southwest of Chesaw and extends to Beaver Canyon on the south and Toroda Creek on the east. Timber and abundant bunch grass were two main attractions that first lured homesteaders to the Pontiac Ridge country.

Around the turn of the century, the Great Northern Railroad promoted homesteading in the hopes of increasing railroad travel. Charles Mooney of Pontiac, Illinois helped arrange for these promotion programs to be held in his hometown, and thus laid the groundwork for his move to the Northwest. When the Mooneys arrived in 1903 and 1904, their only neighbors were the D. J. Wood family. In time, after the available homestead locations had been exhausted, it turned out that practically the entire population in the area hailed from Pontiac, Illinois, thus the reason for naming their new community after their old stomping grounds.

Settlers raised grain, gardens, cattle, pigs, goats, and chickens and milked cows. Agriculture, timber, and mining were the main industries. Several sawmills were also operated in the area. One of the better known mines is the iron mine called the Magnetic Mine on Buckhorn Mountain. Originally, Buckhorn was called Copper Mountain because of the ore there. The Crystal Butte Mine located on the south end of Buckhorn even had a stamp mill on Meyers Creek in the early days. Other mines in the area were Apex, Roosevelt, Gold Ax, and the Iron Ring. The first schoolhouse, a log building, was built in 1906. People who live on Pontiac Ridge today can go both directions to do their trading—Chesaw and Oroville, or Curlew, Republic, and Tonasket.

RIVERSIDE: Community established around 1900. Location: On the Okanogan River, seven miles north of Omak. Center Sec. 25, T35N, and R26E. The town of Riverside came into existence at the mouth of Johnson Creek about seven miles north of the present site of Omak in the early 1900s. This was a logical place for a distribution center, as it marked the head of navigation for steam-wheelers coming up the Okanogan River.

This photo was taken in 1905, when freight wagons crowded into Riverside, the head of navigation on the Okanogan River and supply center for a vast area. (Photo from Okanogan County Historical Society collection).

Riverside was platted in 1902 by James E. Forde. The town was originally known as "Republic Landing" in a thinly disguised effort to convince shippers that the merchandise consigned to the booming camp of Republic could be economically dispatched to Johnson Creek. The steam-wheelers continued to bring hundreds of pioneers into this area. Riverside was ideally located as a supply center. When time came for a boat to arrive, the streets were lined with wagons waiting to buy goods.

In 1913, Riverside had two department stores, a drug store, meat shop, and two hotels—the Occidental and the Cooper. There were lawyer's offices, a shoe shop, a

The last remaining saloon in Riverside.

hospital with two doctors, two restaurants, a dance hall, a post office, church, school, and two saloons.

In the 1920s and 1930s, young people had a good life at Riverside, swimming in and ice skating on the Okanogan River. There were basketball games, music programs, and church functions. The old school building still standing in Riverside was a large part of the town life. At one time, 250 pupils attended. The present school was built in 1914. In 1956, however, the total remaining six high schoolers were transferred to Omak. In 1976, with Riverside's population declining, the grade school was annexed to Omak. Old-timers say the community spirit went out of the town when the schools were shut down.

Riverside today is a town with only a few businesses. There remains a saloon, DeTro's western store, a post office, small store, and a city hall. As people seek out places to live that are still rural and with elbow room, Riverside with its colorful history will never be forgotten.

ROBINSON: Community established around 1900. Location: Nine miles northwest of Mazama at the junction of Robinson Creek with the west fork of the Methow River on Hart's Pass Road. SE Sec. 36, T37N, R18E. The town of Robinson sprang up after the earlier tent town of Ventura, located two miles lower on the road, had died. Ventura lost its usefulness, however, once the road was extended further into Slate Creek. Robinson Creek, 22 miles from Winthrop, was the end of the road and the point of departure for the Slate Creek miners in the late 1800s. For a while, Robinson ranked as a lively little settlement. A hotel and barn were built at the mouth of Robinson Creek along with a freight depot—all to serve the miners. Scattered through the woods in the area was a Methow Trading Company store, post office, blacksmith shop, and saloon.

RUBY: Community established around 1888. Location: Seven miles southeast of Conconully. SE/SW Sec. 29, T35N, R25E. Ruby, or as it was called prior to incorporation, Ruby City, came into existence in the late 1880s. Rich discoveries of silver ore were made in the Okanogan County, and prospectors and miners flocked there in large numbers.

Businesses in Downtown Ruby, 1886–1899

The following is a partial list of business operators and professional people who lived in Ruby from 1886-1899:

Gus Spainhower—Barber
W. Bolinger—Trustee of a general merchandise store
Dr. Graham—Dentist
J.M. Byrnes—Mother Lode Saloon
Della Marshall—Office Saloon
Virginia Grainger—Ruby School Teacher (1892—1893)
Robert Allison—County Sheriff
James Gilmour—Blacksmith and Miner
J.M. and Sarah McKinney—Livery Stable
E.P. Gaillas—Restaurant
Palmer and McGrath—Freighters
Layton S. Baldwin—Attorney at Law
H.M. Marsh—Contractor, Builder, and School Teacher
Henry Carr—U.S. Deputy Mineral Surveyor; Cashier, Bank of Ruby; County Superintendent of Schools
Reiniger and Grieger—The Ruby Brewery and The Saloon
Albert C. Olsen—Okanogan Drug Co., Prescription, Paints, Oils, Etc. Also Agent for State and Transportation Company.
John Stanton—General Merchandise
Dr. C.F. Webb—Medical Doctor; First Publisher of the *Ruby Miner* Newspaper
Isaac T. Keene—General Store of Keene and Hurley
H.M. Keene—Proprietor of Ruby Hotel
T.D. Fuller—Co—Founder of Ruby; Proprietor of Arlington Hotel
W.J. Dorwin—Real Estate Sales; Saloon Proprietor
Thos. Murphy—Shoemaker and Harness Repair
A.E. Shackleford—Livery, Feed and Sales Stable
S. Lichtenstadter—Proprietor of the Bank of Ruby; Real Estate Sales; Liquor Sales; Mining; General Store of Lichtenstadter & Co.
Wm. Stafford—The Silver Corner (Selling Wine, Liquor, and Cigars)
McNall and East—Livery and Feed Stable
J.W. Jewett—The Cheap Cash Store (Selling Dry Goods, Groceries, Hardware, and Miners' Supplies)
W.W. Weeks—Partner in Lichtenstadter & Co.
D.M. Adamson—Livery Stable
Hiram & Laura Huntly—Proprietors of the "Chop House Restaurant"
W. Goettel—Tailor Shop
O.B. Cassell—Snug Saloon
John & Lizzie Bartlett—General Merchandise Store
C.B. Comstock—Leased a Saloon
Nettie Covington—Saloon Proprietor
J.C. Lovejoy—General Merchandise Store (Sold To H.F. Phillips) Manager Of Okanogan Mining & Supply Co.; Second Postmaster of Ruby
H.F. Phillips—General Merchandise Store (Bought from Lovejoy)
R.H. Blevin—Mineral Assayer and Chemist
KcKinney and McNall—Livery Stable
S. Gardner—Blacksmith
F.W. Brown and I.H. Campbell—Tobacco, Fruit, and Newsprint
Charles Leroy—Ruby City Restaurant and Others
Chauncey Carpenter—Sawmill Operator at Southern End of Town
John Singer—Butcher Shop
S. Barnhart—General Store

Photo on the left: Ruby, queen of the cities of the Okanogan mining booms. In 1892-93, Ruby had 29 businesses, including six general stores. (Photo from Okanogan County Historical Society collection). Photo on the right: Only a few stone foundations remain at the overgrown ghost town site of Ruby, where once the population exceeded 700 souls and the Main Street was built up solidly with buildings that stretched for a quarter mile on each side of the street.

Within a brief period, Ruby had become one of the liveliest and best known mining camps in the Northwest. For a quarter of a mile on each side of a single graded street it was built up solidly. An exceedingly busy population engaged in nearly every brand of trade. The mines were located on the high ridge that rises abruptly from the town on the south. Ruby gained a population of several hundred people. A finely equipped and expensive concentrator was built one-half mile east of town, and a wire tram was constructed from the mill to the mines on Ruby Hill, quite a distance away. The citizens of Ruby decided to incorporate in 1890. With the formation of Okanogan County, in March 1888, Ruby became temporary county seat. It continued to hold this honor until February 9, 1899.

On August 4, 1890, a petition was presented to the commissioners asking for the privilege to vote on the issue of incorporation. On August 23, 1890, the proposition for incorporation was carried, and Ruby became a town. The price of silver fell in the fall of 1892. To continue working the mines would be unprofitable, so they were closed down. People moved away, leaving vacant houses unprotected, and the once-flourishing town was depopulated. For some time, the scores of buildings, business, and houses remained solitary and empty, sad reminders of a town that had seen better days. Then came vandals who stripped the houses of all that could be carried away. Buildings, fences, and sidewalks fell into decay, and the city presented a decidedly dilapidated appearance.

If you want to visit a site where once saloons were full, gunfights reportedly were common, and the inhabitants—mostly miners—experienced fires, floods, and the fear of Indians on the warpath, Ruby is definitely the place to go. Today, as you drive past trees lining both sides of the road, all you will see is the indentations surrounded by stones that served as foundations. The trees creak in the wind at Ruby, and perhaps that was the laugh of a miner or the fall of a pick high on Ruby Hill.

RUSSELLVILLE: Community established around 1908. Location: In the hills up Aeneas Creek in the Aeneas Valley. Tucked away among these hills was a settlement called Russellville. H.B. Russell was a land developer who had big dreams for this area. Instead, he provided his clients with many disappointments. Mr. Russell ran his advertisements back east and claimed magnificent homesteads with good water rights, excellent timber, and fabulous possibilities of raising good fruit for the influx of mining people in Republic. His fee for "locating" a homestead was $50.00.

The Great Northern brought newcomers into the country by a special car to Republic. The May 15, 1908, issue of the *Chesaw News* told of the arrival of 20 families that came from Kilbroun, Wisconsin, and drove stakes in the rich Aeneas Valley. Russell, an active and capable leader of the community, had many plans for the new settlement. Part of the plan was to build a road from Riverside to Republic for hauling produce and supplies. His road, called the Russell Road, remains today. Another part of the plan was to build a sawmill for the settlers to market their timber. A dam was built on Aeneas Creek, and a mill site was located downstream. This water-powered sawmill was never completed, however, and the hand-hewn timbers for the foundation were still in evidence a few years back. There was also a creamery, which didn't operate, and a flour mill, which was later moved to Republic.

It soon became evident to the community that their leader was a dreamer and that promises were impossibilities. With some "persuasion" from the settlers, Russell tucked his tail between his legs and left the country. A small handful of these settlers remained for a time, while the rest of the homesteads were soon absorbed into neighboring ranches.

SHERIDAN: Community established around 1897. Location: Sheridan Mountain, east of Toroda. Silver ore was discovered at Sheridan in 1897. W.M. Jennings and Fred Mayes started the Zella M. Mine and, along with others built a reduction mill near the town of Sheridan. The ore was sent down to the mill in a chute built of poles. This chute could still be seen in places about 15 years ago and some of the old mill foundations can still be seen today.

Milling, however, didn't turn out to be profitable, and the mill closed after just a few years, and the people moved away. At its peak, just over 200 people lived in

A few of the original buildings from Sheridan remain today, but even the ghosts have departed.

Sheridan. Rumor was that Lieutenant Phil Sheridan located the Phil Sheridan Mine when he was through the area in about 1880, but nothing indicates this in his reports to the army. A mill was built in 1914, but the recovery was not successful, although a few hundred tons of ore were processed at the Bodie Mill in 1917. The fall of 1917 saw the closing of the Phil Sheridan Mine.

Guy Helphrey, who had a general store in Sheridan, is the only businessman known to be in Sheridan in 1917, although there was a hotel, the remains of which can still be seen today, as can the remains of the Helphrey Store. The mill buildings of the Phil Sheridan Mine are still there. The Sheridan Mine produced $75,000 of silver in its time.

SILVER: Community established around 1890. Location: Five miles southeast of Twisp on the Methow River NW/SW Sec. 35, T33N, and R22E, about three-quarters of a mile from where Beaver Creek joins the Methow River. Silver was the first town established in Methow Valley. It served as a supply center for early settlers.

It had the first post office, the first dances, and the first motion picture show. A saloon, blacksmith shop, and store with dance hall located above. Here the pioneers gathered for all-night hoedowns.

The town was washed away by the flood of 1894. Silver rose again on a flat above the Methow River, but other towns were taking over. In 1900, the famous Red Shirt Mine on nearby Polepick Mountain gave up the ghost. Four years later, Silver did, too.

SWANSEA: Community established around 1892. Location: Upriver about six miles from Virginia City and two miles beyond the mouth of the Okanogan River. NW/NW Sec. 17, NE/NE Sec. 18, T30N, R25E. In 1892, Charles H. Ballard, the Conconully surveyor, platted Swansea on the Okanogan County side, about two and one-half miles downstream from the confluence of the Okanogan and Columbia Rivers. Maps showed streets, alleys, and parks profusely laid out with a flotilla of steamers unloading cargo at wharves served by railroads.

A small store was built and a hotel started. On a flat 60 or 70 feet above the river, the Swansea Hotel was erected and a road built down the steep bank from it to the store. The road was quite steep, however, and no one used it. After only a few months, the Swansea store closed when its proprietors were taken into custody for selling hard liquor without a license. This ended any possible future for Swansea.

SYNAREP: Community established around 1908. Location: Tunk Valley, just above where the county road crossed Tunk Creek.

SQUAW CREEK: Community established around 1889. Location: Methow Valley, one mile up its namesake creek. Squaw Creek, a lower-valley Methow tributary, was the site of the earliest hard-rock mining in the valley. Miners swarmed to the Methow when quartz showing fine gold was discovered in the vicinity of Squaw Creek around 1886.

Every day, several families and many single prospectors joined the mining camp on the north bank of Squaw Creek. W.A. Bolinger came to the little settlement around

1889. He observed the frenzied activity, saw a need, and started a general merchandise store. Then came a blacksmith shop, barbershop, assay office, and a schoolhouse, all within a year.

This mini-mining community eventually harbored four general stores, two hotels, restaurant, saloon, livery stable, meat market, and a sawmill. A five-stamp mill stood on the banks of Squaw Creek, and in 1892, two arrastras operated between the town and the stamp mill. The arrastra was a large piece of equipment used for pulverizing ores containing free gold. After the process was complete, the gold fragments were then collected using mercury. Some of the mines that operated in the area were: Ocean Wave, Exclusion, Paymaster, Second to None, and the Philadelphia. The Squaw Creek gold rush ended as fast as it was born, however, and Squaw Creek turned into a ghost town.

TORODA: Community established around 1897. Location: Four miles northeast of Wauconda. Toroda was once a flourishing little mining camp. Shortly after the opening of the Colville Indian Reservation for mineral entry, people flocked into what was supposed to be an exceedingly rich mining district.

Toroda became a town when gold and silver ore were discovered at Sheridan in 1897. Sheridan was high in the mountains where there were no roads, so the miners built their town along Toroda Creek. Toroda reached its peak in 1898 with a population of 470 people.

Photo on the left: Old Toroda as it looked around 1910, abandoned and left to the ghosts. (Photo from Okanogan County Historical Society collection). Photo on the right: Today, the Toroda of old has all but vanished. The dusty Main Street with horses and freight wagons is no more, although one log building still remains from those historic pioneer days.

There was the Gailliac Hotel, general store, blacksmith shop, butcher shop, eating places, and a post office that was established May 25, 1898. The mines did not prove to be rich as anticipated, however, and the boomtown was deserted. Toroda City soon became known as Old Toroda. A new town called Toroda was begun at the mouth of Toroda Creek on the Kettle River. The name Toroda means "Dorothy" in a local Indian dialect. Both places were named after John Lute's wife.

TONASKET: Community established around 1892. Location: 24 miles north of Omak, 16 miles south of Oroville, and 40 miles west of Republic on the Okanogan

River and Great Northern Railway. Sec. 16, T37N, R27E. Last of the permanent boomtowns to get under way in the Okanogan County was Tonasket, named after the famous upper-valley Indian chief.

In 1888, W.W. Parry opened a trading post on the west side of the Okanogan River about six miles south of present-day Tonasket. There, Parry built a store, saloon, blacksmith shop, a barn large enough for 16 horses and hay storage, and a hotel with 10 rooms. On December 7, 1895 Parry opened a post office and named it Tonasket.

TWISP: Community established around 1898. Originally known as "Gloversville" in 1897. Location: On Methow River, 34 miles northwest of Pateros. Common corner Sec. S 7,8,17 And 18, T33N, R22E. When mineral discoveries were made up the Twisp River Valley, a supply point called Twisp came into being. Soon, its streets were clogged with prospectors heading up the Twisp River Valley or further north, into the Slate Creek Mining District. Twisp grew considerably, and its business district consisted of dozens of businesses. Twisp today is more of a tourist and community town.

Fourth of July parade, Clover Street, Twisp, just before the big fire of July 13, 1924. (Photo from Okanogan County Historical Society collection).

The Alder Mine Mill that still stands today near Twisp was discovered in 1896. It has been one of the most productive mines in Okanogan County, yielding over one million dollars in precious metals.

VIRGINIA CITY: Community established around 1893. Originally known as "Virginia Bills." Location: At the north end of the present bridge over the Columbia River at Brewster and now a part of Brewster, SW/SW Sec. 14, T30N, R24E.

William (Virginia Bill) Covington, who, after a disappointing venture in the Fraser River gold fields, had drifted into Okanogan County in the 1860s, opened a trading post near the north end of the present-day Brewster Bridge. Covington claimed to come from a "first family of Virginia," although his alleged liquor traffic with the Indians, which was illegal, seemed less than true.

Covington's Virginia City attracted the usual businesses, restaurant, saloon, livery stable, blacksmith shop, and eventually a hotel from materials torn from the unused Swansea Hotel and two abandoned saloons at Conconully. A half-mile north of Virginia City, a better ferry landing and safer tie-up for a floating steamboat wharf were located on John Bruster's homestead. There, yet another town was platted. Thirty-two heads of horses pulled Gamble's Hotel to the new site, which became known as Brewster.

WAUCONDA: Community established around 1898. Location: Twenty-two miles northeast of Tonasket, 17 miles northwest of Republic. NE Sec. 10, T37N, R30E. This is one and a half miles southwest of the site of Old Wauconda. The first Wauconda came into being in 1898, after a wide ledge of quartz carrying free gold in it was discovered. This discovery touched off a headlong rush into the area as prospectors envisioned another Eureka Camp.

By 1898, a substantial community had grown up around the mine. Before long, a general store, three crude hotels, four saloons, and a handful of other businesses catered to the miners' needs. By 1901, a post office opened, and Wauconda was on the map. The town soon claimed a population of 300.

On June 14, 1917, the Wauconda Community Hall was dedicated. Fifteen hundred people attended the big celebration, coming from Ferry and Okanogan counties.

By 1901, the mine was showing signs of depletion as the ore began to dwindle away. Soon after the mine closed down, Old Wauconda met its death. The towns-people, however, simply picked up and moved westward to a new site two miles away. The second Wauconda never matched the status of Old Wauconda. It had a school, post office, several places of business, and a growing population of homesteaders. A new highway between Republic and Tonasket was laid in 1929, which bypassed the second town of Wauconda. J.R. VanSlyke picked up stakes in 1930 and moved his store and post office to a new site close to the new highway. Today, the last Wauconda stands by Highway 20, not far from the original sites.

Deserted old homestead from the pioneer days of yesteryear.

In every direction in Wauconda, history beckons the history buff. To the north lie old abandoned ghost towns like Bodie, Old Toroda, and Sheridan. The hills and mountains are covered with abandoned mines, and close to Wauconda scores of abandoned log cabins and old deserted pioneer homesteads can be found. Don't miss seeing the old Pflug mansion south of Wauconda in a grassy draw close to the road.

WEHESVILLE: Community established during the 1880s and 1890s. Location: Wannicut Lake area, in a remote canyon valley. In the summer of 1886, a strip of land 15 miles in width and bounded on the north by British Columbia was neatly sliced from the Columbia Indian Reservation. This bit of rocky land, long fought over for its purported mineral wealth, was taken from Chief Moses and returned to public domain. Dubbed Fifteen-Mile Strip, droves of miners came by all manner of means into the rugged hills. During the '80s and '90s, family travel into the new land was dangerous, due chiefly to the hazardous road conditions. Revelries, settlements, and little shanty-and-cabin towns were soon formed.

Among the new arrivals were five men from the same family. They were Prussian and had the gloom of Napoleonic wars in their heritage. Their grandfather was a drum major in the battle of Waterloo. The oldest member coming here was Frederick, who was dubbed "Major" Wehe, a distinction he earned in the Civil War. A snow-white beard covered his chest; he was gentle and well liked in the pioneer community. He came in 1891, bringing a son, Eugene, and soon showed up with others: George, Albert, and August.

The Wehes built a great mining mill in this location and called it Wehe Consolidated Mining and Milling Company. It soon grew into a town named Wehesville. The land, however, was not altogether given up to mining. It also grew as a farming community, and here and there on the benches and draws where springs existed there were scattered ranches upon which crops were grown, chiefly oats and wheat. A poor crop occurred around 1917, and with alarming persistence, the same failure also happened the following year and the next.

The end had come. Wehesville became a deserted town to which arriving ranchers used the lumber for their own use. Only one building is left today—the company office. A hundred years later, hikers enjoying the nice trails and vistas find little traces of early habitations. Even where the great mining mill once roared, there are no traces, only memories.

WINTHROP: Community established around 1890. Location: Forty-four miles northwest of Pateros at the forks of the Methow and Chewuch rivers. SW Sec. 2, T34N, R21E. In the 1890s, Winthrop was transformed from a little-known stopping-off place to a bustling distribution point. Like most of Okanogan County towns in those days, mining activity was the fuse that ignited its growth. In 1891, Boston-bred Guy Waring, his wife Helen, and his three stepchildren, Harry, Robert, and Anna Green, arrived in the Methow Valley and established a trading post at the forks of the Methow and Chewuch Rivers. Charles Look, postmaster, who lived on the river about one mile south, had already named the settlement after the early western explorer, Theodore Winthrop. It is also known that the town was named after John Winthrop, the colonial governor of Massachusetts, for reasons that are unclear today.

One can mosey on down this classic Wild West town of Winthrop's Main Street today and never know it was once one of the great mining towns of the Methow Valley.

On April 1, 1892, Waring became Winthrop's postmaster and moved the post office to his store. It is known that the new postmaster tried to change the name of the town to "Waring," but was turned down by the postal department.

Waring's Harvard classmate, Owen Wister, a writer of Westerns, spent his honeymoon here in 1898. People believe that he gathered material for his popular book, *The Virginian*, here, inspired by the rustic beauty.

Waring's enterprises consisted of large land holdings, including the first commercial orchard, Land Five, in the upper valley and also a small sawmill on the bank of the Chewuch. Guy Waring hated liquor, but, liking money, he opened the Duck

Brand Saloon and excessive drinkers were abruptly "given the boot." A policy that must have surprised (but sobered) many patrons.

In the spring of 1868, placer gold was discovered in the Slate Creek District. Although the placer discoveries drew hundreds of miners into the new district, it was the later discoveries of lode mines that kept them there. By the 1890s, with prospectors pouring into the region, Winthrop gradually assumed the role of a staging point. When Colonel Tom Hart built a road 34 miles into the Slate Creek area, Winthrop's future was guaranteed. In 1901, the town of Winthrop was platted by the Methow Trading Company. By 1915, most of the mines, except for a few in the Slate Creek area, had shut down. Winthrop was hard hit, and it gradually declined in importance as its population plummeted.

It struggled through the Depression years amidst rumors that it was destined to become a ghost town. In 1972, the North Cascade Highway opened, and Winthrop changed its appearance. Merchants united with the help of local lumber baron, Kathryn Wagner, to restore the town back to its original early Western mining look. Winthrop today is alive and well and prospering. The old town has been restored, and a surprising number of original false front buildings still stand along its Main Street. Today, tourists who visit Winthrop will see how the town has retained the mood of yesteryear.

Originally known in the old days as Winthrop Billiard Parlor, this structure stands today as the landmark Three-Fingered Jack's Saloon.

GHOST TOWNS OF
CHELAN COUNTY

This county has long been considered to be one of the most scenic counties in eastern Washington. This region has an intriguing history and it has changed very little since the turn of the century.

Lake Chelan, which is one of the major attractions of this county today, remains a breathtakingly beautiful expanse of water. It has become a major resort area, and many of the large old Victorian houses of early pioneers still stand today.

The once-famous mining camp of Old Holden, where prospectors and miners mined gold, silver, and other ore for so many years, is no more. The old community of Stehekin still prevails today, 55 miles west of the town of Lake Chelan, at the headwaters of this lake.

There is little mining activity on those once-boasted-about streams. There are still places within this county that almost remain unchanged, one of which is the Blewett Pass region in the southern part of this county. Miners returning from the Fraser River strikes in British Columbia discovered the first Swauk placer gold in 1858.

AZWELL: It is unknown when this community was established. Location: Above Wells Dam. Azwell was a small community on the Columbia River that grew from the business success of Alfred Z. Wells and his nephew, Alfred Morris. Owners of a hardware store in Wenatchee, they enlarged into the orchard business as a sideline, then discontinued their partnership in 1914. Wells kept the orchard business; Morris kept the store. Azwell became a company community for several years.

CAMP CHELAN: Near the east side of town on private land just off State Route 150.

This small settlement lasted only for a short period because it was near the Moses Columbia Reservation, newly established for the Chelan, Methow, Sinkiuse, Entiat, and Wenatchee Indian people. The Army felt as though it should be close by to protect the white settlers from possible attack by the Indians and vice versa. The reservation lasted only a few years and then was returned to public control with the agreement of Chief Moses. There is no evidence of the Camp Chelan site today.

CHELAN: Community established around 1881. Location: South end of Lake Chelan on Hwy. 97. The earliest settlers were Chinese placer miners who were mining the bars on the nearby Columbia River as late as the 1870s. They remained until local Indians drove them out. By 1881, the United States Army had established Camp Chelan, and several years later, the first settlers started coming. Among the early arrivals was William Sanders, a prospector who was convinced that the upper regions of Lake Chelan held large bonanza riches in minerals. Later on, vast mineral discoveries were made on Cascade and Railroad Creeks and further beyond, on the head of Lake Chelan. Eventually, the mighty Holden Mine became one of the greatest state producers, and provided millions of dollars worth of precious metals during its long life.

HOLDEN: Community established around 1896. Location: Eleven miles above the west shore of Lake Chelan.

STEHEKIN: Community established around 1880s. Location: Nestled beneath the high mountain peaks at the head of Lake Chelan.

Miner's carbide lamp. The reservoir at the top was filled with water; the bottom was filled with carbide, which would then activate a flame. These were sometimes attached to a miner's helmet. Before the carbide lamp came along, the miner's used what was known as the candleholder, or "Sticking Johnny," which was used in mines as a means of light.

GHOST TOWNS OF
FERRY COUNTY

The boomtown days have vanished into history and so have the bonanza years of the mining era. In towns like Curlew, Orient, Republic, and Danville, however, the sounds of those glory days and bonanza times can still be heard in the echoes of yesteryear.

Cowboys and miners on their horses and wagons no longer stir the dust in the streets as they did over a century ago. The old stamp mills, some still standing today, no longer thunder their echoes in the hills as they did back then. Gone from their old haunts are the miners, prospectors, Native Americans, and pioneers.

Sit back, relax, and enjoy your historic adventure back to the days of yesteryear in Ferry County.

BELCHER CAMP: Community established around 1899. Location: Ten miles northeast of Republic on upper Lambert Creek. The name Belcher Camp is rarely spoken of today, even in Ferry County. There were many more mining camps in the state during its boomtown days, but few were as unique as Belcher. At its peak, the population was only 72, and it wasn't even a gold camp—its miners mined iron. Around 1897, a large body of high-grade iron ore was discovered. By 1906, Belcher was a complete mining camp. It had a post office, large bunkhouse for single miners, general store, five or six cabins, and a railroad. Eventually, the mine shut down, the camp was abandoned, and today, there isn't much left to mark its passing.

CURLEW: Community established around 1900. Location: At the junction of Curlew Creek and the Kettle River. Late in 1896, shortly after the opening of the north half of the Colville Indian Reservation to mineral entry and homesteading, two adventurous traders set up a general store at an old ferry crossing. This trading post rapidly sprouted into a collection of log buildings and stores. By 1901, the community had a population of nearly 200 and claimed two general stores, two saloons, the Ansorge Hotel, two livery stables, a dry goods store, and several other businesses. A post office had been established in 1898, and the town was designated Curlew. The early years were a booming time for Curlew as the region was flooded with prospectors, miners, railroad workers and Indians attracted to a new frontier. However, Curlew never really got off the ground. It seemed to stand still after those hectic first years. The minerals failed to live up to those early expectations and the dreams of

Curlew slowly faded. The Ansorge Hotel is still there today, although many of its false-fronted buildings are long gone.

DANVILLE: Community established around 1889. Originally known as "Nelson"
Location: Just south of the Canadian line. This town is rarely spoken of in the archives of Washington's history, although it ranks up front among other historic mining camps in the area. Its mines, some of which produced impressive amounts of high-grade ore, survive today. Danville was the first town in Ferry County. The Nelson brothers established it in 1889. In 1896, it became a congregating place for prospectors anxiously waiting for the north half of the Colville Indian Reservation to open up for mineral entry. By 1897, Danville had half a dozen businesses, post office, and one of the first newspapers in the county.

In 1901, when the Washington and Great Northern Railroad built a railroad through Nelson, their officials had the name changed to "Danville" to avoid confusion with Nelson in British Columbia. While the mines were giving up the ore, Danville thrived, but by the end, Danville slipped in importance as activity slowed. In the 1920s during Prohibition, Danville, like Nighthawk, Chesaw, and Molson, became a smugglers rendezvous. Much whiskey was smuggled across the border and into the surrounding areas. Today, Danville still occupies that large flat where Nelson was first established so many years ago.

FERRY: Community established around the late 1890s. Location: Northwest of Curlew.

Ferry was founded during the late 1890s. It was thrown up almost overnight—a ramshackle collection of crude log and false-front buildings bordering a dusty Main Street. It got its share of traffic during those early years, most of it heading north into British Columbia and Alaska. When the mining boom slowed, however, so did the town of Ferry. By 1910, it was on its way out, and before, long Ferry passed into history.

Today there is hardly a sign of that once-busy camp; some depressions remain where once a building had stood.

ORIENT: Community established around 1900. Location: On the Kettle River.

Three prospectors, Maloney, Morri, and Dunkle, discovered the Never Tell Mine, a surprisingly rich deposit of free-milling gold ore. This triggered a stampede of prospectors and miners into the region. Just across the river, a temporary camp the miners called "Orient" because of the Oriental placer miners that had once mined the bars of the river decades before, gave this settlement its name. Within months, numerous mines were producing spectacular ore. By 1905, mines like the First Thought, which produced a staggering $180,000 in ore, mainly gold, had put the town on the map. Around 1910, the Orient State Bank opened up for business. It had a school, town hall, and a newspaper.

The prosperity of most boomtowns in Northeastern Washington was dependent on the mines. Orient was no different. When the price of silver and gold dropped, it had a dramatic impact on the town. It was the beginning of a long, slow decline. By the 1940s, despite occasional flurries of mining activity, Orient was little more then a stopping place.

REPUBLIC: Community established around 1896. Originally known as "Eureka."

Location: South of Danville on the Kettle River. In early 1896, Tommy Ryan and Phil Creasor, both tramp prospectors, were persuaded by three businessmen to check out rumors that somewhere on the upper San Poil was bonanza gold. As the two prospectors traversed into the area, they followed the Kettle River from its mouth as it looped back into Canada. It was a long route, but it skirted the Kettle River Range, an obstacle of high wilderness and deep snow.

Finally, on February 28, they reached their destination and started searching for that bonanza gold. They noticed a promising looking draw, and a short time after entering it, they discovered a massive and continuous mineralized ledge. They soon staked out over 10 claims just in this area alone.

When rumors of the great strike got out, a swarm of prospectors began to flow into the area. A mining camp gradually began to develop. The area here was soon referred to as Eureka Gulch. Soon the entire area was overrun by hordes of prospectors and miners. When high rollers like Patsy Clark and others began buying up mines and shares in the area, it was the making of a boomtown.

By 1900, it had more then 20 saloons, seven hotels, nine general stores, three newspapers, bank, opera house, and many other businesses. On June 3, 1899, a huge fire swept along Clark Avenue and left more than half of the business district in ashes. By 1910, Republic was still a busy boomtown, but its decline seemed to be approaching with the ore trade slowly declining in volume and threatening the very existence of the town. In that same year, however, a virtually unknown mine called Knob Hill came into production. The Knob Hill Mine became the greatest gold mine in the entire state of Washington and one of the most famous producers in the United States, yielding a staggering total of close to 2,400,000 troy ounces of gold during its lifetime. At today's gold prices that would be around $640,800,000.00.

Troy Weight

In calculating the weight of gold and silver, a different scale, called "troy weight," is used. Troy weight is figured differently from the usual avoirdupois weight, which is the common standard used in calculating the weight of articles other than gold and silver.

20 pennyweights = 1 troy ounce

5,760 grains = 12 troy ounces

12 troy ounces = 1 troy pound

24 grains = 1 pennyweight

480 grains = 20 pennyweights

GHOST TOWNS OF KITTITAS COUNTY

Passing images of yesteryear still remain close by in this historic county where names like Easton, Roslyn, Cle Elum, Salmon La Sac, and a handful of other coal-mining camps of old come to mind. Travel along the deserted trails or rivers like the Cle Elum or the Teanaway, and you will be following the paths of prospectors and miners who entered into these remote areas in search of gold.

OLD BLEWETT: Community established around 1896. Also known as "The Camp" in the early years. Miners returning from the Fraser River strike in British Columbia discovered the first Swauk placer gold in 1858. By the 1860s, Blewett was home to over 200 miners and prospectors. It had a reputation as one of the most disorderly and violent mining camps in Chelan County.

When the quartz veins proved to carry great amounts of "free gold," the gulch was stampeded by miners and prospectors as word spread throughout the county. In 1879, a wagon road was built to connect the camp to the outside regions. By 1878, a stamp mill had been built to process the ore. By the 1890s, mining companies like the Blewett Company were employing more and more miners and the camp began to expand. There was a busy hotel, general store, twenty-stamp mill, livery stable, two saloons, post office, and several shacks and cabins for miners.

Most signs of this once-historic boomtown have yielded to time, fire, and highway construction, but the stone foundation of the old stamp mill remains. Old "glory holes" still honeycomb the mountains throughout this area. Many of these old mines can be seen from U.S. 97 that winds through this rugged country.

BLEWETT

GOLD! In 1860, when word of its discovery spread, prospectors rushed to pan the gravels here in Peshastin Creek. A century ago, 200 to 300 people lived and worked in this narrow valley. The town of Blewett once stood around this very spot.

By 1874, the early placer workings had played out, but veins of gold had been found. This brought on a boom of hard-rock mining. Thousands of feet of tunnels were burrowed into the hills. In 1879, the mining district was connected to the outside world with the construction of a wagon road to Cle Elum.

The community was called Warner with establishment of a post office in 1893, but the name was changed to Blewett later that same year. It was named after Edward Blewett of Seattle, whose Gold Mining Company controlled many of the claims. Buildings included a school, two-story hotel and boarding house, stores, saloon, telegraph, frame and log homes. A road to Peshastin was completed in 1898, and stage lines ran three days a week.

Along U.S. State Route 2, about 23 miles north of the turn off to Liberty, is this historical roadside marker where the mining camp of Old Blewett once stood.

CLE ELUM: Community established around 1883. Location: Just off I-90, east

Photo on the left: The old boom town of Blewett in the late 1890s. By the 1860s, Blewett was home to over 200 miners. Hardrock mining soon followed the placer operations, and the camp added a hotel, boarding house, and mercantile store to its larger cluster of shacks. The 20-stamp mill can be seen at the right and the hotel on the left. Photo on the right: Not much remains today of old Blewett's 20-stamp mill.

of Snoqualmie Pass. The economy of Cle Elum has managed to keep pace with changes in railroading, coal mining, and saw milling. It now depends primarily on logging and recreation.

The Native Americans referred to it as the "beautiful valley," but what ultimately spurred white settlement of the upper-county communities of Cle Elum and Roslyn was something dark dug out of the ground—coal.

Although rich in Native American history and lore, the northern portion of Kittitas County was not the home of year-round Yakima Indian settlements. The Yakamas did frequent the area during the summer months to fish and pick berries.

Cle Elum (which means "swift waters") traces its history to 1881 and a pair of friends from Pennsylvania, Walter J. Reed and Thomas Gamble.

Gamble, a prospector, traveled through the region and, upon a chance meeting with Reed in Yakima, told him of the beauty and possibility of rich resources in the area. Reed and his wife, Barbara, traveled to northern Kittitas County from Yakima and were immediately taken with the territory.

In the spring of 1891, Reed filed a preemption claim of what is now the original town site of Cle Elum.

In 1894, Reed and Pete Brosious discovered coal in what is now Roslyn. In fact, coal created the boom towns of Cle Elum and Roslyn. By 1905, Cle Elum's population was 1,500 and eventually reached a peak of 3,000. Reed and his wife envisioned Cle Elum as "another Pittsburgh." Cle Elum steadily declined in population through the century, however, as the coal mines closed and the timber industry dwindled.

Cottages built for miners and mill workers give residential streets a homogeneous, turn-of-the-century appearance.

Cle Elum has Barbara Reed to thank for its broad streets. The wife of the founder of this town was determined that the town should have this amenity. The Reeds lobbied the approaching Northern Pacific Railroad to build a depot on their land and even offered the company half of all profit from lot sales in their newly platted town site.

EASTON: Community established around 1888. Location: Along I-90 east of Snoqualmie Pass. Easton developed as a logging camp. The arrival of the Northern

Pacific in 1888 increased activity in lumbering as opportunities for shipping expanded, and in 1909, the rails of the Chicago, Milwaukee, and Puget Sound railways crossed the Northern Pacific rails here. Railroad workers increased the population. Easton was the last station where trains could be serviced before going over the Cascade Mountains. In 1934, the town experienced a severe fire. Today, the town of Easton boasts a beautiful setting adjacent to Lake Easton and the state park.

LIBERTY: Community established around 1880s. Also known as "Williams Creek" and "Meaghersville." Location: Just east of Hwy. 97 on Blewett Pass Hwy. It's the oldest mining town site in Washington. Originally established as "Williams Creek" in 1880, it was renamed "Meaghersville" in 1887. In 1912, the post office was moved from Old Liberty on Swauk Creek to Meaghersville, and the town was called Liberty in accordance with post office regulations.

An old deserted prospector's cabin from the mining days of Liberty.

In more than a century, its miners have mined more than three and a quarter tons of placer gold. The Liberty Historic District has been placed on the National Register due to its exceptional American history of the past. Liberty is the oldest mining town site in Washington State and possesses exceptional value in commemorating American history. Today, the present town site of Liberty still stands beside famous Williams Creek as it has for more than 131 years—a tribute to the mining days past.

RONALD: Established around 1886. Location: About three miles northwest of Roslyn.

Ronald is the sister town to Roslyn. Ronald had its own coal mine, saloon, school, and store, but many of the people would travel to Roslyn to shop for goods.

In 1886, just before railway crews began to build the rail line across Stampede Pass, the Northern Pacific Company brought in around 400 Italian immigrants to open a coal mine called #3. Two years later, during a hostile strike, angry men attacked mine foreman Alexander Ronald (for whom the town is named) and left him bound to the tracks just outside of town. The story goes that in the boom days, miners had a still for brewing whiskey in the basement, and when things got too hot, they would hide it in one of the mines in the area until things cooled down.

Several of the original buildings line Pennsylvania Avenue in Roslyn today and are over one hundred years old. They were occupied by saloons, billiard halls, a barbershop, and wash houses. After the coal miners had finished cleaning up after a hard day's work in the mines, they could then go to the brothels on the upper floors.

ROSLYN: Community established around 1886. Location: About three miles northwest of Cle Elum. In a lot of ways, it's a classic Western mining town and has kept a certain personality of its own that few other historic towns in Washington possess.

Drive down Pennsylvania Avenue and the boomtown of yesteryear Roslyn stands before you. Original false-fronted stores line the once-busy avenue, complete with fading wood and decor from the past.

In 1886, a prospector looking for gold named Nez Jensen and a traveling blacksmith named George Virden found a mountain of coal southwest of Cle Elum Lake. At that time, there was a tremendous demand for coal because the railroads were looking for large quantities of it. A partnership soon took over the vast holdings of Jensen and Virden, and by the end of the year, the Roslyn coal mines were in production.

Photo on the left: The Roslyn Café was originally a meat market in 1887, called Hartman's. The top floor was the VFW, and the sandstone used to construct this 1887 structure came from the surrounding area. The mural of a camel advertising the Roslyn Café has been a focus of attention for tourists since the mural was featured in "Northern Exposure." Photo on the right: Roslyn was the filming location for the fictional town of Cicely, Alaska in the hit television series "Northern Exposure."

Soon a mining town began to take shape. It was a rough camp in those years, inhabited by hundreds of hard-core coal miners who played as hard as they worked. Before long, the camp became a boomtown and what a boomtown it was! Saloons had control of the business section of town. By 1901, the population reached the 3,500 mark, production of the mines passed 1,000,000 tons for the first time and the town was booming. Then in the 1920s, the demand for coal began to taper off, and by the late 1920s Roslyn was beginning to fade.

The Roslyn of today is not just known for its historical importance as a coal-mining town.

In the summer of 1990, the television series "Northern Exposure" choose Roslyn to be "Cicely, Alaska."

Those that remember Roslyn as a bustling coal town consider it fortunate that their town was selected to be "Cicely Alaska." Thanks to "Northern Exposure," prosperity has returned to Roslyn.

Roslyn Cemeteries Tell a Historical Story

The Old City Cemetery is the oldest cemetery in Roslyn, founded in 1885.

The Roslyn cemeteries are on the "must see" list for every visitor that comes to Roslyn, as they are truly unique.

You'll find 25 separate ethnic and fraternal lodge cemeteries making up this outstanding feature of Roslyn's pride and culture. The groups of cemeteries are clustered on the mountainside and cover approximately 15 acres. Most of the various nationalities and ethic groups, which made up the population of early-day Roslyn, are represented in the cemeteries.

Headstones follow the custom of European cemeteries. In European cemeteries, a photo of the deceased is on the headstones as well as the ethnic group to which the deceased belonged. In addition, many of the graves appear to be above ground due to the fact that the grave sites are on a steep, sloping hill, when in fact they are not above ground at all.

GHOST TOWNS OF PEND OREILLE COUNTY

This easternmost county in Washington State is little traveled even today. There are several places in this county that have rarely been traveled since the boom days of the mining era, places like Divide Peak, Lead King Hills, Sullivan Creek, Hoaknoee Mountain, and many others. These town sites are quiet today, although there was a time over a century ago when every prospector and miner knew their names.

CUSICK: Community established around 1900. Location: Northwest of Newport about 20 miles on the west side of the Pend Oreille River. In 1903, Cusick opened its post office—a mark of success for any pioneering community. The name was derived from the Cusick brothers, Joe and Frank, who owned and operated a fleet of five sternwheelers that carried freight, passengers, and mail. Around 1910, train largely replaced steam wheelers.

The rail connection to the outside markets brought prosperity as men logged virgin white pine and processed it through the lumber mills. Today, the present economy depends on construction work and local service companies plus newsprint and aluminum-fabricating plants.

DALKENA: Community established around 1900. Location: About 12 miles northwest of Newport. Dalkena was a logging town, and what a logging town it was! Up until the 1930s, a busy railroad station handled hundreds of passengers and millions of board feet of lumber to be shipped. The old river pilings protruding from the Pend Oreille River are witnesses to the many log booms that once supplied local mills for decades.

Two Great Lakes lumbermen, Henry Dalton and Hugh Kennedy, choose a small community called Glencoe as the town site for a new company town. They constructed a large sawmill and called it "Dalkena" as the name, a combination of the first syllables of their last names. Dalkena consisted of mill offices, two bunkhouses, cookhouse, and general store. Surveyors laid out three city blocks to handle businesses and homes.

IONE: Community established around 1880s. Location: About 15 miles south of Metaline Falls on the west side of the Pend Oreille River. Steamwheelers began arriving here in the late 1880s, although regularly scheduled stops didn't start happening until after a post office opened in 1896. In 1910, an engineer from England located limestone in the area useable for making cement and opened a processing plant, which operated only a few years. Until the late 1930s, lumber was an important industry for Ione, and it had one of the largest mills in Northeastern Washington.

NEWPORT: Community established around 1892. Location: Close to the west border of Idaho on Hwy. 2.

TIGER: Community established around 1880s. Location: Four miles south of Ione.

USK: Community established around 1892. Location: About 17 miles northwest of Newport.

GHOST TOWNS OF
STEVENS COUNTY

There are long-forgotten places in this county that time has passed by. There are also places that still remain today, such as Marcus, Leadpoint, Northport, and Addy, where history has stood still and the mood of yesteryear lingers on. These were the days when mining was the talk of the town. The echoes of miners at work can almost be heard, and the chances of striking it rich are still in the thoughts of many whom visit this historic county.

ADDY: Community established around 1900. Also referred to as "Addy Station." Location: Seven miles northwest of Chewelah, just a few hundred yards west of Highway 395. You might not know it's even there, but don't miss old Addy; it's been there for almost 100 years.

It was called Addy Station once, and there was a time when it was a distribution center with some importance. That was when the Spokane Falls and Northern railways made regular stops here, and mines in the area were shipping hundreds of tons of rich silver ore. Eventually, however, the mines gave up the ghosts, and Addy, like so many other boomtowns also played out. Addy still has several old buildings of historical importance, and the surrounding area still recalls the time of those bonanza days.

BOSSBURG: Community established around 1897. Location: Northern Stevens County, on the southern side of the Columbia River. In the late 1890s, Bossburg was the great transportation center of Stevens County. Ideally located on the southern side of the Columbia River, it commanded routes in all directions. By 1901, it had a population of 600, and the town was still growing. It included numerous freighting outfits that transported all types of mining supplies and machinery to boomtowns in the various counties and British Columbia. It became such a scene of action, it claimed two telephone companies, a newspaper, town hall, two ferry companies, three saloons, three general stores, and two hotels.

Bossburg existed only as long as the mining boom. And when the mines gave up, the town wasn't far behind. Today, it would be hard to realize that a boomtown had ever existed here.

BOUNDARY: Community established around 1899. Location: Northern Stevens County, close to the Canadian line. For a few wild months, it was a hell-rais-

Beautifully engraved stock certificate from the famous Boundary Red Mountain Company issued in 1923. This historic document has an ornate border with a vignette of an elk.

ing, redneck camp on the northern edge of the frontier. Its single main street was lined with false-front buildings, most of them saloons.

In its height in the 1890s, the camp population soared to almost 900. It was a typical railroad camp then with all of the crude entertainment of the day: bare-knuckled fights, all-night hell raising, and drinking designed to separate the construction men from their hard-earned wages.

In its declining years, the Boundary Hotel, post office, general store, and a few souls inhabited the site. When the railroad finally spanned the savage Pend Oreille River with a bridge, "New Boundary" came into being south of the original town site.

Today, there remains only a deserted and dusty flat, but a closer examination reveals the faint traces of the first town site. Overgrown depressions where basements once stood and rows of rocks outlining old building sites still remain today after more then a century.

CEDARVILLE: Community established around 1897. Originally known as "Cedar Canyon." Location: Deer Trail District of southern Stevens County in a remote canyon deep in the mountains northwest of Spokane. Six miles east of Fruitland were two successful mines. A town sprung up nearby full of miners and people to supply the miners with food, clothing, and shelter. This town was

Cedarville. There were over 300 men working at the Cleveland and Deer Trail mines. A post office was established in 1909. The town was also known as Cedar Canyon, Chloride or Deer Trail.

There were four saloons, a store operated by Mr. Diamond, and a log house that served as a hotel. In 1900, there was a stage to Springdale and Fruitland. The surrounding land was rich, and many settlers raised produce and meat for the miners. Cedarville had a school that was in session for two months in the spring and two in the fall. The teacher lived in the back room of the school building. After the mining boom was over, most people left Cedarville or moved to towns in the surrounding area.

Cedarville in its early days, also known as Cedar Canyon, Chloride, and Deer Trail.

CHEWELAH: Community established around 1890. Location: Seven miles southeast of Addy. This boomtown started during the 1880s after the Old Dominion Mine had been discovered east of nearby Colville. In 1883, silver and lead deposits were discovered at Embry Camp. In a short span of time, over 20 strikes were made in this area alone. However, the strikes soon petered out, Embry Camp soon vanished, and Chewelah took over as its own. By 1910, Chewelah had a population of nearly 1,500 with a wide Main Street bordered by handsome buildings. Unlike other mining boomtowns, the mines around Chewelah kept producing ore well into the 1950s. Today, those mines are nothing more then holes in the ground and lie silent with their stories of the past.

COLVILLE: Community established around 1883. Location: About 25 miles northwest of Chewelah.

KETTLE FALLS: Community established around 1889. Location: About 10 miles northwest of Colville on the east side of the Columbia River.

LEADPOINT: Community established around the early 1890s. Location: Located in the mountains southwest of Northport. Leadpoint is a little-known mining camp located in the northern part of Stevens County. It derives its name from the high-grade deposits of lead ore, which were discovered in the early 1890s in the nearby mountains. Leadpoint became the main distribution center for many of the mines in the area.

It came into its own around 1915 when a trapper decided to take a look at a spot where lightning continuously struck near the same spot on a mountain. He explored this area and finally located a large tree blackened and split by numerous lightning strikes. He noticed several pieces of lead ore lying on the ground around and near the tree.

Several months later, a fellow prospector examined the lead ore samples and determined that it was of high-grade lead. The next day, the two of them set out to locate the lightning scarred tree. Luck was with them that day, after several hours of searching the mountain they not only located the lightning tree but also an incredibly rich vein of galena (high-grade lead ore). On July 2, 1915, they recorded their claim and named it the Electric Point. The Electric Point became one of the most fabulous mines in Stevens County, producing millions of dollars in profits.

Mostly on the strength of the Electric Point, Leadpoint grew to a respectable population of nearly 200 souls. It had a hotel, general store, barbershop, and a few other businesses.

Not much remains today. A few old abandoned structures with their weathered boards are about all that is left near the old town site. Even the ghosts have surrendered and departed.

MARCUS: Community established around 1885. Also referred to as "Old Fort."
Location: About five miles north of Kettle Falls on the east side of the Columbia River.

It was ideally located to command the steam-wheeler traffic on the Columbia River. Every trader, trapper, pioneer, and prospector heading into the upper Columbia region passed by Marcus.

It wasn't always known as "Marcus." When the fur traders dominated the northeastern area, it was known as "Old Fort." Later, it came to be called "White's Landing." When a distinguished trader named Marcus Oppenheimer opened a general store that controlled the town and prospered in a big way, the town became known as "Marcus," and the name stuck. When Oppenheimer arrived in 1863, he realized that the site was centrally located and that Marcus could benefit from this. But it was a long wait for Oppenheimer. It was 1885 before it was given post-office status, when its population was holding at 50.

However, the town slowly began to live up to its expectations. By 1910, its population skyrocketed to nearly 300. The gold and silver mines on both sides of the Columbia River were yielding hundreds of thousands of dollars' worth of precious ore, and this, coupled with renewed confidence after nearly 10 years prosperity, made firm the position of Marcus. Those bonanza years eventually declined as the silver and gold was depleted. The gloom intensified when the once-great Northport Smelter finally closed.

So Marcus, like other boomtowns in upper Northeastern Washington, moved into the Depression years. But the greatest shock was yet to come. It was announced that Marcus would be flooded by the rising waters of a new lake created by the completion of Grand Coulee Dam. In 1940, after the completion of the dam, Marcus slipped into its grave beneath the waters of the mighty Columbia River.

Today, there is a new Marcus, high on a bench above the original town site. It's a neat little town, but it doesn't quite have the style of that first Marcus.

NORTHPORT: Community established around 1890. Location: Northeast of Bossburg nestled between the base of a high cliff and the Columbia River. Over the years, Northport has suffered a series setbacks, including fires and a depression, but somehow it has managed to survive.

Northport, like many of the boomtowns in its day, was founded on the energy and dreams of miners and prospectors seeking their wealth in placer gold. In 1890, on Red Mountain in British Columbia, north of the Columbia River and just across the Canadian border, two prospectors from Spokane made a series of discoveries. The two mining prospectors, Joe Moris, and Joe Bourgeois, soon staked their claims.

Inland Empire Railroad quickly sized up the situation. By 1892, construction gangs were hard at work laying track along the south side of the Columbia River to a site 15 miles below the Canadian border. In 1892, D.C. Cobrin, renowned railroad builder, purchased this site, which became known as Northport. In 1892, a passenger train arrived at Northport pulling behind it a flatcar with a post office and a saloon loaded on it.

In early 1893, a fire swept through the business district, reducing it to ashes. It was the first of many fires to hit Northport and a first of a series of disasters to haunt the town.

Northport and mill in its early days.

This disaster was short-lived, however, and by 1896, Northport was really coming on strong. The north half of the Colville Indian Reservation had been thrown open to mineral entry, and hundreds of miners and prospectors stampeded in to seek gold.

Buildings were going up everywhere, as everyone wanted a piece of the action. By 1895, the mines in the area were producing ore at such a flurry that the Le Roi Smelter was constructed to refine the ore from the famous Le Roi Mine and others. A railroad bridge had been constructed across the Columbia River, and the railroad had reached the boomtown of Rossland, the famous "Golden City" of the Canadian west, and ore began to arrive into Northport smelter.

But the boomtown days of Northport were nearing an end. The Le Roi management sold their interest in the smelter to a Canadian investor, and much of its custom ore, now being refined on the Canadian side, began to slip. The once-thriving community began to decline. Businesses began shutting down. The final blow came on the morning of July 29, 1914. The greatest fire in Northport history leveled almost the entire business district. Northport would not recover as it had in the past. A gloom settled over the town and worsened when the smelter finally shut down and was dismantled. By the 1930s, the glory days of Northport were history. The original smokestack from the smelter still stands today as a monument of those days gone by.

SPRINGDALE: Community established around 1890s. Location: About six miles off I-395 north from Spokane to the Canadian border. The junction is at Loon Lake about 37 miles north of Spokane. The old road that Springdale is on also goes through the town of Valley, Washington and junctions with I-395 again just before the town of Chewelah.

Springdale had a little bit of everything: farming, logging, and mining. The Deer Park Lumber Company started the town. Mining was a little east of town towards Hunters. The mines were known as the Cleveland mines and mined lead, silver, cadmium, and several other minerals.

At one time, there were "Wanted Dead or Alive" posters of Wyatt Earp, Virgil Earp, and Doc Holiday for claim jumping there.

The town at one time had a creamery with a doctor's office on the top floor, granary where farmers could take their crops into be ground and sacked, several saloons, mercantile, barbershop, boarding house, train stop, blacksmith, livery stable, post office, and a sawmill. There was a marshal's office and a one-cell jail. One unique feature was a tavern/saloon for Indians. There was another one for whites. Several of the original buildings are still standing today, and the Springdale Community Center has entered them on the historical register. Just outside of town the small cemetery has legible stone markers going back to 1892 and a number of wooden and unmarked graves that could date back even further.

A Brief History of Native American Peoples of Northeastern Washington Region

What is the History of the Native American Peoples of Northeastern Washington?

What are the Colville Confederate Tribes?

For hundreds of years before explorers and settlers reached the lands of the Columbia Plateau, numerous tribes of native people occupied the territory of eastern Washington.

Up to mid-1850s, the ancestors of the Colville Confederated Tribes were nomadic. Life changed for them, however, with the coming of settlers. Today, the Colville Confederated Tribes are made up of 11 different bands of Indians. Ten bands are from eastern Washington State, and one band, the Nez Perce, is from northeast Oregon. The 10 bands are Wenatchee, Entiat, Chelan, Methow, Okanogan, Nespelen, San Poil, Lakes, Moses, and Palouse.

How did these Native Americans live?

As nomadic peoples, the different bands hunted different sources of food according to the season. Deer and other big game plus dried salmon were the primary food of winter. People lived in the mountains in small groups. In the spring, the native people congregated in slightly larger groups to gather camas and other roots in the lower valleys. Through the summer and fall, the Columbia River provided abundant numbers of salmon and other fish, which encouraged large concentrations of Salish-speaking people. Most of the Indians of eastern Washington, northern Idaho, northwestern Montana, and the lower interior of British Columbia spoke related languages, thus the language was collectively referred to as "interior Salisham."

How did the different bands come to be called the "Colville" tribes?

Many different tribes fished and traded goods with each other in the area of Kettle Falls, Washington. In the 1820s, white people learned that the Indians excelled at trapping and stalking game for the large fur trade. For this purpose, a man named Simpson established a new fort at Kettle Falls.

Hudson's Bay Company, Fort Colville, Washington in 1888 showing stockade. At the far left is the blockhouse. (Northwest Museum of Arts & Culture/Eastern Washington State Historical Society, Spokane, Washington.)

The new post was to be called Fort Colville, after the leading member of the committee of directors in London, Andrew Wedderburn Colville. Colville was in the rum and molasses business, but never set foot in America. He had, however, advanced Simpson to his position of leadership. Thus, the form of homage.

Trading took place at Fort Colville almost daily. From 1826 to 1887, Indians traded beaver, brown bear, black bear, grizzly, muskrat, fisher, fox, lynx, martin, mink, otter, raccoon, wolverine, badger, and wolf pelts. Beaver and otter were most important, but martin and bear became popular after the 1840s. As many as 20,000 pelts a year went out of Fort Colville.

As time went on, and for convenience, the term "Colville" became more and more to be used as a designation for the native people of this area. Because of Fort Colville, all neighboring bands were eventually confederated as Colville Indians. By executive order of President Ulysses S. Grant on April 9, 1872, the Colville Indian Reservation was formed and became the permanent home to the Indians. St. Paul's Mission near Kettle Falls today includes the original site of Fort Colville, once the second largest center for fur trading in the Northwest, and a rustic log missionary church.

When were the boundaries of the Colville Reservation established?

The original reservation was in existence for less than three months in 1872, when other executive orders and agreements began to take portions of the reservation for public domain. Over a 10-year period the Colville Indian Reservation was reduced to its present size, less than half of the original.

How big is the Colville Reservation?

The Colville Indian Reservation is 2,300 square miles—about 1.3 million acres. It is bigger than the state of Rhode Island.

How many people are in the Colville Reservation today?

More than 8,200 people are members of the Colville Confederated Tribes as of 1999.

How is the reservation governed today?

The Colvilles are a sovereign nation governed by their own administrative and judicial branches within the boundaries of the reservation. Leading the tribal membership is a 14-member business council elected from the four reservation districts of Omak, Nespelem, Keller, and Inchelium.

Where is the tribal government located?

Tribal headquarters are located on the Colville Indian Agency campus near the town of Nespelem.

What kinds of businesses do the Colville Tribes operate?

Timber and wood products are at the heart of the Colville Tribes' multimillion dollar industries. Overseeing the $100 million in tribal business ventures on the reservation is the Colville Tribal Enterprise Corporation (CTEC). There are about 2,000 people employed on the reservation. In addition to its timber operation, CTEC operates a sawmill near Omak, Washington, and a state-of-the-art wood treatment plant at Inchelium. The tribes also have a nursery to replant and grow trees. The tribal fish hatchery stocks all the lakes and streams in north central Washington State.

What are some of the cultural and religious practices on the reservation?

Proud of their heritage, the Indian culture and religions are very much alive and active on the Colville Reservation. There are the Seven Drums and the Indian Shaker religions as well as the Indian winter Chinook Dances, the annual spring thanksgiving Root Feasts, and the memorial giveaways in honor of the deceased.

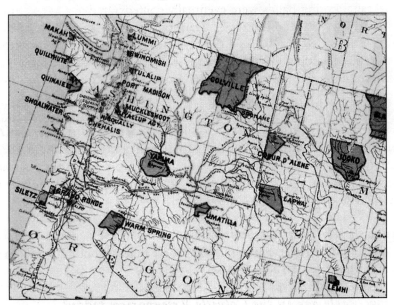

Map showing Indian reservations within the limits of Washington State circa 1890. (Northwest Museum of Arts & Culture/Eastern Washington State Historical Society, Spokane, Washington.)

THE LEGEND
OF THE HEE HEE STONE

Six and one-half miles west of Chesaw on the old stage coach road from Republic to Oroville and Conconully is the legendary Hee Hee Stone. Once a shrine, the stone is now a crumbling ledge of rock, difficult for history buffs to locate. There have been many mysterious legends connected with the Hee Hee Stone, handed down from generation to generation. Tales of the Hee Hee Stone were once filtered through the smoke of Indian tribal councils, and even today, the stories of this rock are still told around fireplaces on winter evenings.

The historical site of the legendary Hee Hee Stone. Supposedly white prospectors under the influence of liquor dynamited it to pieces the night after Labor Day 1905.

According to legend, the Indians along the Okanogan became infected with a disease not unlike leprosy that threatened to destroy the whole Indian nation. The medicine man of the Siwashes (the generic term for all Indians) talked every day with the Great Spirit, who told him to tell his people that he would send a spirit to talk to them. On a certain day, all of the people were to gather at the place named to receive the messenger of the skies.

On the appointed day, Indians came from hundreds of miles to see whether or not the medicine man had told the truth or was only dreaming. Early in the morning the medicine man pointed toward Mt. Bonaparte, and thousands of eyes looked in that direction. Soon an image began to appear in the southern skies, assuming the form of an angel, and before the astonished Siwashes could fall to the ground and pray, the heavenly spirit had alighted upon the Hee Hee Stone.

She was radiantly beautiful and began to talk to the afflicted people. She told them that the Great Spirit had heard their cry for help and that she had come to help them. She motioned all that were suffering from the epidemic to come near her and be healed. Within a short time, the afflicted were transformed into a host of shouting Siwashes, rejoicing in the perfect health that had been given them.

The medicine man explained to them that she would come again some time in the future, but that they must use the means that she would provide if they wanted to retain their good health. She distributed camas seed among them, which became an important staple of the Indians, and urged that they be planted everywhere, the roots of which when eaten would prevent a return of the disease from which they had suffered. She wished them to be of good cheer, to deal fairly with one another, and that some time she would come again. While the shouts that greeted this announcement were echoing over the hills, she was caught up in the air and disappeared in the southern skies in the direction from which she had come. Ever since, she has been known to the Siwashes as Queen Camas, the divine spirit from the sky that healed the people. The Indians have never ceased to worship this rock, invariably leaving something upon it as they pass by.

INDIAN AMBUSH AT MCLAUGHLIN CANYON

The best-known historic Indian battleground in Okanogan County lies at the south entrance to the legendary McLaughlin Canyon, a few miles southeast of Tonasket. In this remote canyon in the summer of 1858, Indians who were nervous over white intruders entering their lands attempted to ambush a party of miners heading for the Caribou gold fields, lead by David McLaughlin. One of the men in the McLaughlin party was Francis Wolff, a merchant and experienced Indian fighter. Only a handful of accounts of the ambush have come to life over the past 143 years. One of the least-known recollections is that of Francis Wolff. He was born in Pennsylvania on June 15, 1833 of German parentage.

In the spring of 1857, with 18 miners whom he had supplied with goods, Wolff started for the Frazier River gold fields, teaming up with David McLaughlin's party in Walla Walla. The McLaughlin party consisted of 160 miners, traders, packers, and several hundred pack animals. On July 20, 1858, the party left from Walla Walla for the newly discovered gold fields on the Thompson and Frazier Rivers. The gold discovery on the Thompson and Frazier Rivers was made by William Peon and an Indian chief of the Frazier River Indians on a small creek running into Thompson River, about ten miles above its mouth, called the Necoman Creek. In 1857, Peon brought five hundred dollars' worth of gold dust to the Colville Valley and disposed of it, which created the great excitement and stampede into the area.

McLaughlin and his party outfitted themselves and headed north to the gold fields. These were not greenhorns stumbling northward; but rather were seasoned experienced wilderness travelers. The parties took up the line of their travels north across the Columbia plateau along the Columbia River and to the mouth of the Okanogan River and Fort Okanogan—a trading post of the Hudson Bay Company unmolested by the Indians.

As they approached the edge of the river, they saw bands of Indians on the other side and called to them for canoes to cross the river with supplies, but the Indians paid no attention to their demands. After waiting for a half a day, one of McLaughlin's guides came across the river with a chief called Pieere. They were told that the Indians objected to them crossing the river and for them to go any further, they would fight before they would allow the party to continue. After consultation, Francis Wolff was selected to cross the river with Montune as the interpreter. After talking all night, the Indians agreed for a consideration (supplies) to cross, with the assurance they would not fight them.

After crossing the river with the Indians assisting them with their canoes, David McLaughlin appointed an advance and rear guard of 25 men each. They made a three-day march up the Okanogan River without seeing an Indian. When the reached the sand and gravel bars of the Okanogan River, near the mouth of what we know today as McLaughlin Canyon, they noticed many footprints coming and going. They became concerned that the Indians were near, and were expecting a serious assault. McLaughlin halted the advance guard until all the party was together. Then they started through the canyon, which is a narrow passage 40 to 100 feet wide, with shear vertical walls hundreds of feet high on each side. These widen at the mouth of the canyon to some 200 yards. They had proceeded about 100 yards when McLaughlin and his guide noticed dry wilted bushes and wondered if the bushes had been torn up to provide camouflage. Thinking it strange, he went to examine the bushes when the Indians behind it fired. The shot hit McLaughlin's horse in the neck, and the animal fell, McLaughlin diving behind it. The shots came from the side and rear of the canyon with the Indians trying to drive the party deeper into the canyon. Men jumped from their horses, and those not killed or wounded returned fire. Francis Wolff's horse, which had $2,000 worth of gold dust in the saddle bags, got away from him and ran up the canyon about 75 yards in the direction of the attack. He went for his horse, got him, and returned to the firing line. Three of McLaughlin's party were killed and three wounded, but history shows no Indians were killed. If the wilted bushes behind which the Indians were lying in ambush on

Looking south down McLaughlin Canyon in the direction the attack took place. Okanogan River is in the distance.

MCLOUGHLIN CANYON

UPSET BY AN INCREASING FLOW OF MINERS HEADING FOR BRITISH COLUMBIA GOLD FIELDS, INDIANS LAY IN AMBUSH THROUGH THE LENGTH OF THIS CANYON ON JULY 29, 1958, AS 160 MEN LED BY DAVID MCLOUGLIN APPROACHED FROM THE SOUTH. THE WARRIORS HAD CAMOUFLAGED THEIR STONE BREASTWORKS WITH BRANCHES BUT WILTED LEAVES ALERTED MCLOUGHLIN'S ADVANCE PARTY SO THE INDIANS OPENED UP PREMATURELY. FIRING CONTINUED FOR SEVERAL HOURS NEAR THE MOUTH OF THE CANYON A HALF-MILE BEHIND THIS SIGN. THREE WHITES WERE KILLED. THE CARAVAN RETREATED TO THE OKANOGAN RIVER AND NEXT DAY CROSSED OVER ON RAFTS.

This sign erected by the Okanogan County Historical Society stands high above the cliffs of the legendary McLaughlin Canyon.

both sides of the canyon had not attracted McLaughlin's attention and that of his party, I doubt if anyone would have gotten out alive.

More About David McLaughlin: The Man in Charge

He was the youngest son of the Hudson's Bay Company's northwest manager, John McLaughlin, and his part-Indian wife Marguerite.

David McLaughlin was born in 1821 at Fort William on Lake Superior. He received further education in Montreal, Paris, and London, where his father enrolled him in the East India Company Military Seminary.

McLaughlin worked for Hudson's Bay from 1840 to 1849. His experiences included a fur trapping expedition to California in 1844-45. However, his interest lay in mining. He resigned from the Hudson's Bay Company and reportedly recovered $20,000 in gold dust over five months. This led him, at 37, toward the Fraser River mines and into the ambush. Following these adventures, McLaughlin spent most of his remaining years farming near Porthill, in northern Idaho. He married Annie Grizzly, daughter of a Kootenay Indian chief, they raised nine children.

Better-educated than his neighbors, McLaughlin taught school as a volunteer and kept the first weather records at Porthill. He died at 82 in 1903.

David McLaughlin in his later years. (Photo from Oregon Historical Society collection.)

BOOM TOWN STORIES

BOOM TOWNS AND GHOST TOWNS

Some ghost towns just refuse to give up the ghost!

The once-booming town of Molson is such a town. Founded in 1900 by George B. Meacham (promoter) and John W. Molson, (investor) Molson's population quickly grew to 300.

While its inhabitants may have abandoned the town, memories of Old Molson's glory days still linger in the weathered buildings of a ghost town that just refuses to give up the ghost.

John Molson, owner of the largest brewing company in Canada, as well as The Molson Bank, which boasted branches in every province throughout the country, invested heavily in the town. The Molson Town Site Company built many of the buildings that housed those early businesses. Within the first year a newspaper sprang up, as well as three general stores, a drug store, three saloons, a dance hall, livery barn, blacksmith shop, assay office, an attorney's office and a doctor's office. There was also a three-story hotel (the hotel Tonasket-named after the great Okanogan Indian chief of the same name) that included a two-story outhouse.

When prospecting failed to bring in the expected revenues, the Molson Company pulled its backing and moved on. The town's population dwindled even faster than it had grown and by 1901 there were only 13 people still living in the town.

Homesteaders began moving into the surrounding area by 1903 and although the town didn't change too much, the stage did make regular scheduled stops and settlers began to trade goods and services with town members.

Sometime before 1905, J.H. McDonald filed on 165 acres for a homestead, 40 acres of which encompassed the land the Molson Town Site Company had developed into the town of Molson. Early in 1905, the railroad announced their intentions of laying tracks through the town, and Molson started filling again. On April 15, 1909, McDonald posted notice that any person living, residing, or doing business on his tract of land (which included the entire town of Molson) must vacate immediately.

When Molson's citizens were unable to obtain clear titles to their property, the decision was made to found a new town near the railroad tracks – New Molson was built half-mile to the north. While New Molson flourished, Old Molson quickly faded away. While its inhabitants may have abandoned the town, memories of Old Molson's glory days still linger in the weathered buildings of a ghost town that just refuses to give up the ghost.

Original site of Old Molson's marshal's office and jail house.

THE MYSTERY OF RICH BAR

A stampede was triggered in October 1859, when soldiers of the Ninth Infantry guarding the American commission panned for gold from the Similkameen River at Rich Bar, about one half mile upstream from the later site of Enloe Dam.

Rich Bar is now submerged beneath Enloe's backwater. Its exact location is uncertain, but there has been evidence the bar was just downstream from Shanker's Bend. Over 31,000 ounces, a total of more than 2,500 pounds troy, came from this locality, mainly from Rich Bar itself. It was an astonishing find, but some of those early prospectors knew that the origin of the gold lay close by.

By the late 1890s, serious attempts to locate the mother lode were being made. These prospectors, most of them old hard-rock miners, knew that there was a vein or series of veins just upriver from Rich Bar and these veins had been the origin of the massive amounts of bonanza placer gold that had been recovered by earlier miners.

The old theory that it had broken away from a hidden vein and had been carried down river eons ago and had lodged just downstream of Rich Bar is generally accepted.

In the early days of mining, every prospector and miner was a potential millionaire, drawn by the whispers of "bonanza gold" in the mountains, hills, and streams of Northeastern Washington State.

Shanker's Bend with Rich Bar in the foreground were well-known placer gold deposit locations on the Similkameen River. The undiscovered "Rich Bar Vein" is still sought after today by treasure seekers.

A GHOST IN RIVERSIDE?

The Riverside cemetery has a legend attached to it. There's a grave on the far side, which, according to legend, contains the remnants of Frank Watkins, Riverside's only murder victim.

The story goes that angry ranchers had run Frank Watkins, a gun-toting cowboy, out of Oregon. He arrived in Riverside in 1903 with a string of hot-blooded horses having many mixed brands. That night, Watkins entered the saloon and ordered up his favorite drink, a "Tom and Jerry." Jack Williams, the owner of the saloon, told him that he had no more hot water for Tom and Jerrys.

Watkins pulled out his six-shooter and shot the spout off of the kettle sitting on the wood stove. In the crowd was a man, carpenter by trade, who had his saw in his hand, when he heard the shots, he yelled and threw up his hands. Watkins disarmed him of his saw and, before leaving the saloon, put three bullet holes through the ceiling. The one time saloon is now a small grocery store, and the three bullet holes are still there.

The following spring, Frank Watkins met his death. After riding into town, the desperado rented space in Kendall livery stable for his horse and himself, then rolled

Photo on the left: The final resting place of gun-toting cowboy Frank Watkins. Tombstone inscription reads: Laid to rest outside the town cemetery after he was shot to death in a Riverside livery stable about 1904. He just had too many horses in his corral. Photo on the right: These three bullet holes from Frank Watkins' six shooter can still be seen today in the ceiling of the former saloon, now a ma and pa store, in Riverside.

out a gunnysack to spend the night. No one ever learned who shot Watkins. He had been shot right through the sacks with a single wound to the head, killing him as he lay sleeping.

When morning came, nobody in Riverside was sorry to hear that this desperado was dead, and the local townspeople didn't want him sleeping in their cemetery, either, rubbing elbows with their righteous kin.

The former saloon where the desperado Frank Watkins did his drinking is now a small grocery store in Riverside.

His grave is located about 500 yards outside the cemetery on top of a lone hill to the south of the cemetery. The restless ghost of gun toting Frank Watkins is said to have haunted the Riverside cemetery for the last 95 years because the town folks wouldn't let him be buried in their cemetery.

MILLION-DOLLAR ALDER MINE

The history of the Alder Mine near Twisp does not have the legends and lively stories attached to it as was associated with Squaw Creek, Montana, Gilbert, and Red Shirt claims. Yet the Alder Mine has been one of the most productive mines in Okanogan County, yielding over one million dollars in zinc, silver, copper, and gold.

In 1939, in less than eight months, the Alder Group Mining company and its lessee, the Methow Gold Corporation, have received in net smelter returns $228,660 for ore and about $6,000 for concentrate from Tacoma smelter.

In the years between 1950 and 1953, this mine was Okanogan's leading gold producer. The mine shut down in 1953 after producing over $850,000 in gold.

The source of this ore was a vein a few feet in width at the surface and 30 to 40 feet wide on the No. 2 tunnel level. Width estimates up to 60 and 75 feet were also reported. For years, men were said to have tripped on the outcrop and passed on.

In 1896, while panning near the mouth of Alder Creek, T.H. Culbertson found traces of gold. Culbertson kept working up the creek until he came to an outcropping rich in minerals. Later, this site became the Alder Mine. A large stamp mill was built near the mouth of Alder Creek, and this mill and mine operated off and on over the years. When the price of zinc fell the mine shut down.

Abandoned million-dollar Alder Stamp Mill located southwest of Twisp—a mute reminder of the bonanza-mining boom of long ago.

THE PFLUG MANSION: FROM DREAMS TO MEMORIES

This intriguing, old, deserted mansion is nestled in a small ravine surrounded by low grassy hills on three sides. It is located just north of Highway 20, less than one half-mile west of the present day Wauconda store and post office. There is a pull-off next to Hwy. 20 to park and view the old mansion, which is on private land.

John and Anna Pflug came to America in the fall of 1900 from eastern Germany, where they were born. John Pflug had a dream of building a beautiful German-style house for his growing family. He started building his dream home in the summer of 1908. Money was scarce in those early years for homesteaders. He hired no help, doing all the carpenter work himself and hauling the lumber from Turpen's sawmill on Bonaparte Creek, about ten miles away, with a team and wagon. His German-style home was never completed. Like most of the early homesteaders, he found that all he could do was to take care of his family and send their children to school.

John Pflug passed away in Spokane in 1956, and Anna two weeks later in Wilbur. They had ten children, but two passed away in infancy. The Pflug mansion has remained deserted since 1921, a reminder of the dreams our pioneer fathers before us once had.

The abandoned remains of the Pflug mansion near Wauconda.

THE LIFE AND TIMES OF GUY WARING

On July 1, 1884, a Boston-bred and Harvard-educated gentleman named Guy Waring set out from New York with 500 dollars, a wife, and three stepchildren, determined to find success and happiness in the west.

He first settled in Portland, Oregon, holding down a job as clerk in the Comptroller's office of the Oregon Railway and Navigation Company. After only six weeks, Waring lost his job. He decided to abandoned business entirely and try his hand at farming, as he had sprung from a long line of Connecticut farmers on his father's side of the family. Waring thought that perhaps he possessed some small hereditary advantage in this direction.

Waring borrowed 5,000 dollars from a friend back east and, leaving his family behind in Portland, started out to explore the country. After exploring the Puget Sound region without much success, Waring returned to his family, who at this time were wintering in Port Townsend.

Fortunately, Waring found a boyhood friend, Charles E. Peabody, stationed at Port Townsend as a Special Agent of the Treasury Department with the entire territory of Washington as his field. Charles told Waring of a region lying east of the Cascade Mountains, a land of wonderful climate, with cold winters and hot, dry summers. It was the region of Okanogan. This was no finer cattle country to be found in any part of the west, and he assured Waring he would be making a great mistake not to take a look.

This engaging description of this wonderland he had discovered gave Waring's curiosity no rest. Finally, overcome with a desire to see for himself, Waring set out for the Okanogan country.

Waring purchased a ranch in the Okanogan Valley from a gentleman by the name of Wellington. He settled down with his family and began raising cattle. After a few years at farming, Waring met Julius Allen

Guy Waring in 1881, age 23.

Loomis, who convinced Waring to form a partnership with him and go into the storekeeping business. Waring was respected for his puritanical standards, his inflexible honesty, and his outspoken remarks. By the less worthy, however, he was less well liked, because of precisely these same qualities. It was unusual to deal with a storekeeper who warned you against what you were proposing to buy as being inferior in quality and not worth its price. He sold groceries, dry goods, hardware, candy, and ammunition; and he was capable of telling a customer what he thought of him.

Waring's ranch house in the Okanogan Valley near Loomis around 1884.

As shootings among the new settlers and miners became more and more common, it was Waring's belief that it would be necessary for him to take his family away from Okanogan before something serious happened. Loomis agreed to stay and look after the ranch and store, and Waring, in turn, assured him that he was willing to retain a financial interest in the ranch and store if he so desired. He promised Loomis that if the situation should ever improve, he would return. In 1888, Waring and his family moved back to Boston.

It only took four years of renewed living in Boston to convince Waring that the simplicity of life on the frontier was more desirable and more wholesome, and, finally, more rewarding. And so, in 1891, Waring returned to the west. In the Methow Valley, forty miles to the west of his old ranch, he built his new home in a region that, happily, had not been corrupted by the miners.

On September 26 of that year, he established a "squatter's right" on the fork where the Chewuch River flowed into the Methow River. Only about 60 pioneers lived near the forks, and the entire population of the Methow Valley was only about 150. Quick to recognize a potential market, Waring contacted friends in Boston, who loaned him $4,000. Waring spent $3,500 on goods for the community and another $500 on building a dwelling for his wife and young children. On October 10, 1891, Waring began selling and trading merchandise from his wagon. Not until 1897 in Boston, however, did he actually incorporate his business—the Methow Trading Company.

In 1891, Waring actually managed to make his venture pay in its first year, but in 1893, a fire destroyed most of his inventory. With $728 worth of goods saved from the fire, another settler named Earl Johnson became manager. He made a profit for the Methow Trading Company for the next 16 years.

In the years following 1894, Guy Waring diversified his interests throughout the Methow Valley. His business included a small sawmill capable of milling 10,000 feet of lumber daily, an orchard, a water power system, the Duck Brand Saloon, and a freight company.

In 1897, Guy Waring built a rugged, sturdy, hand-hewn log cabin overlooking Winthrop and dubbed "Waring's Castle." The cabin and its outbuildings are now the home of the Shafer Museum. The Simon Shafer family maintained Waring's cabin until it was taken over by the Okanogan County Historical Society in 1976. In 1982, it was placed in the National Register of Historical Places, as one of the nation's cultural resources worthy of preservation.

In 1929, after more than 20 years in his business venture in Okanogan County, his investments were failing. The demands upon him took its toll, and conditions grew unfavorable. In November 1929, Guy Waring boarded the Cunard liner *R.M.S. Lancastria* and headed home to Boston. Guy Waring died at his home in Hyde Park on March 27, 1936, of a stroke.

OKANOGAN COUNTY'S MYSTERIOUS "CHINA WALL"

Arlington Mill, that mysterious set of massive granite walls in the Loup Loup country, on the side of Ruby Hill, is referred to by many as the "China Wall." The great stone walls rise from the heavily wooded slopes of Ruby Hill—walls up to three feet thick, the huge blocks of granite tightly fitted and the corners perfectly squared. The largest of the ten walls measures 80 feet long and 27 feet high. The second is 77 feet long and 20 feet high. This massive structure, one of the most enduring and mysterious of Okanogan County's relics.

Jonathan Bourne, a Portland lawyer obsessed with mining fever, bought a total of 27 claims near Ruby in 1888. Heir of a wealthy New England whaling and manufacturing family and member of Portland's high-class Arlington Club, he soon had a chokehold on more of the mining district than anyone else. No stamp mills existed at this time in the area, but Bourne seemed to know that ore would have to be concentrated before mine owners could afford to ship it to smelters far away. Bourne decided to do something about the situation.

In 1889, he sent a mining engineer to inspect his claims. The engineer reported no mineral signs in several of his claims, but this made no difference to Bourne. He

Photo on the left: The Mysterious "China Wall." This wall is the largest of ten walls, measuring 80 feet in length and 27 feet high. Photo on the right: Strong willed, vigorous, and pulsating with ambition, 23-year-old Jonathan Bourne Jr. was a key figure in the construction of the "China Wall." (Photo from Oregon Historical Society collection).

began to build a brickyard close to the intended mill site. To build the massive granite walls, Bourne hired a German stonemason named Chris Stazman. Stazman organized local miners, carpenters, farmers, and others into a work force that successfully quarried granite outcrops from above the mill site. This same workforce skidded granite blocks downhill, some weighing several hundred pounds, and other single blocks weighing in excess of 2,066 pounds, slightly more than a ton, and built the massive walls using the block-and-tackle method.

During the three-month period of construction of the Arlington Mill, it employed a work force of well over 150 men. The mill was partially constructed during September, October, and November of 1889. It was never finished, however. Jonathan Bourne's Arlington Mining Company was skidding into bankruptcy. The wooden superstructure was torn down, and whatever equipment had been delivered to the mill site was removed.

Only the massive granite stone walls are left today, victims of miscalculation and of the collapse of the silver mining boom in 1893. The original mining claims that Jonathan Bourne had purchased in 1888 on Ruby Hill, the "First Thought," and four other claims and mine, became known as the Arlington Mine. These mines were owned under various owners after Bourne had departed. This shattered any hopes of the Arlington Mill ever operating.

The Arlington Mine was worked briefly in 1905 and again in the early 1920s. In 1936, new owners built a mill at the mine site high on Ruby Hill. There were a total of 15 or 20 men employed at the mill at that time. In 1937, Jonathan Bourne Jr. was 82 years old, living in retirement in Washington D.C. One might wonder whether, Bourne was aware that in distant Okanogan County, an Arlington Mill finally had started operating. Through the years, the massive granite walls have been shrouded in mystery and peppered with speculation.

Somehow the walls have been linked with the Chinese. A number of local pioneers had heard Chinese were involved in their construction. However, a sampling of names on the Arlington Mill payroll records does not show any of a Chinese flavor. Nor does it appear that "Scottish masons" built the walls. This has been one of the most enduring rumors attached to this massive granite structure.

The walls and the rest of the Arlington Mill were constructed by the only sort of work force one might have expected to assemble in the raw, rugged Okanogan County of 1889—miners, farmers, carpenters, masons, common laborers, and drifters.

Rising awesomely from the forested hillside of Ruby Hill and the charming Loup Loup Valley, brooding over unfulfilled destiny as the seasons past, the great granite walls are their monument to history gone by.

How to Get There

The Arlington Mill is located in the Loup Loup area of Okanogan County.

The simplest way to reach it is to turn off the Loup Loup Highway (SR 20) onto the Loup Loup canyon road leading to the Rock Creek campground. The junction is about eight and one-half miles from the south city limits of the town of Okanogan.

On the way, you will pass the Rock Creek campground and picnic area on your right, both operated by the Department of Natural Resources. After about seven miles, on your left will be Antoine Ritchie's sagging cabin. You will cross Loup Loup Creek here.

About .3 of a mile this side of the Arlington Mill is a white post with survey data on it. The granite rock quarry from which the mill was built is directly uphill from this post.

The massive granite walls are not easy to see from the road. They are about 75 to 100 yards up Ruby Hill (to your right). Please respect the private property in this scenic valley for others to enjoy.

From Beginning to End:
How the Arlington Mill Would Have Processed Silver

Washington has a great variety of mineral deposits, and mineral production and processing is one of the major industries of the state. Mineral deposits are distributed throughout the state, but more are concentrated in the northeastern counties. Many of the deposits, as in other areas, are either to small, too inaccessible, or too low in grade to be mined commercially at the present time, but increased prices and improved mining and processing methods undoubtedly will make it feasible to mine more of these deposits in the future.

Most of the Okanogan's gold and silver was secreted in mountains. This required tunneling to get at the ore and concentrating mills to reduce the volume shipped to smelters. Most mills stair-stepped down hillsides so gravity could move materials through the process. The end result would be silver concentrates placed in bags for shipment to a smelter, which would produce marketable silver bars.

The cross section on the following page shows the type of process-concentrating mill the Arlington Mining Company may have been planning.

How Arlington Mill may have looked if completed.

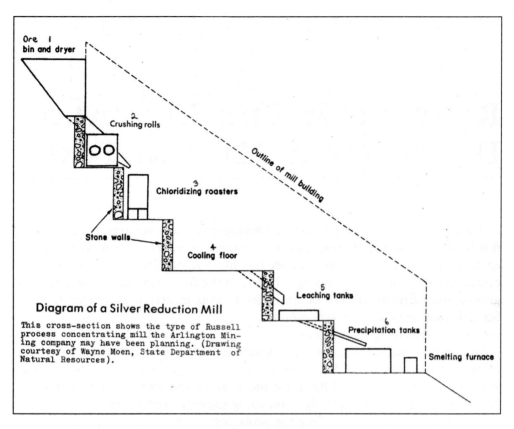

Diagram of a Silver Reduction Mill

This cross-section shows the type of Russell process concentrating mill the Arlington Mining company may have been planning. (Drawing courtesy of Wayne Moen, State Department of Natural Resources).

1. Where mineralized ore rocks from the mines were dumped into the ore bin for processing.

2. Crushing rolls or heavy stamps "rising and falling 60 times per minute with thunder and clatter," making the mill tremble, crushed ore-bearing rocks into smaller pieces. Larger pieces were recycled back to the crushing rolls or stamps; smaller pieces dropped through screens into a settling bin.

3. In the settling bin, filled with water, the rock pieces were mixed with chemicals, causing silver to float to the surface.

4. Silver particles were scooped off the top of the settling bin and moved to an amalgamation pan where they were mixed with further chemicals to remove impurities. The material then flowed into a settling tank.

5. In the leaching tanks, silver tended to sink, while impurities tended to float to the surface.

6. Finally, the precipitation tanks were drained and the silver concentrates placed in a smelting furnace. From here, the silver concentrate was placed in bags for shipment to smelters, which would produce marketable silver bars.

RUBY CITY: THE LIFE AND DEATH OF A MINING TOWN

Thirteen miles north of the town of Okanogan on Salmon Creek there is a place that is probably most aptly described as a wide spot in the road. There are two markers to tell the traveler that this was once the site of Ruby City. In all probability, the casual observer might drive through the site of the town without realizing he is on ground once-famous as one of the chief mining centers of Washington State. Scraggly pine trees have grown up on the site, and heavy shrubbery is slowly covering the few remaining foundations.

Yet, upon closer scrutiny, the place is unmistakable. Through what was once the center of the town runs a road still in use today. There is little doubt that this road was once the Main Street of Ruby, for there can still be seen faint traces of fully a dozen excavations in a fairly straight line along the road. The remains of several rock foundations can also be seen. In a few short years, a lively mining town had come into being, lived, and died. More then 114 years have gone by, but the famous mining camp has become little more than a legend.

Ruby City was not the center of the first mining excitement in the Okanogan country, for there were two earlier mining rushes. Later, mineral discoveries led to the settlement of Moses Reservation March 1, 1886, west of the Okanogan River. As a result of these discoveries, the third mining rush occurred, and a number of camps sprang up in what is now Okanogan County. There is some doubt concerning the exact time and manner of beginning of Ruby. It is possible that miners had squatted in the vicinity previous to the normal opening of the reservation. Thomas D. Fuller, in 1885, built the first cabin on the site of Ruby.

Following the opening of the Moses Reservation, the first mineral discoveries were made in the spring of 1886 on Ruby Hill—a steep mountain rising to the height of 3,800 feet above the town. Ledges of quartz carrying silver and a small quantity of gold were found in the country rock of granite and gneiss. John Clonan, Thomas Donan, William Milligan, and Thomas Fuller made the original discoveries. They struck a ledge about 18 feet wide, which ran uniformly from wall to wall in gold and silver. Here they located the Ruby Mine. It proved to be the lowest-grade mine on the hill.

Thomas D. Fuller and others organized the Ruby Mining District in 1887. First, only a few claims were staked out. Then, almost magically, more people poured into the town. The late '80s saw Ruby in its heyday.

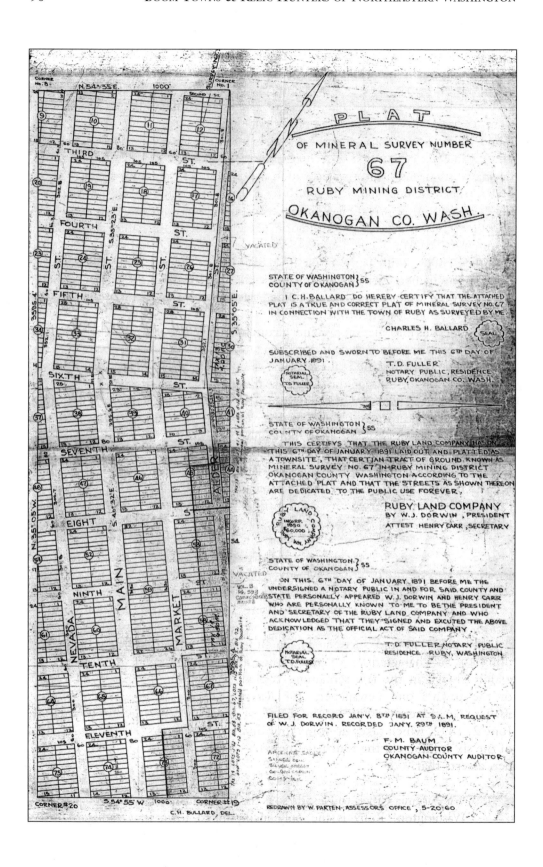

Just how rich was the mining district? Was it justified in the claims made for it? Many stories are told of its richness, but they are not compatible with the early decline of the camp. Most of the mining was done for silver and a small amount of gold. In the reports of the state geologist, the principal mines in the Ruby district were described at length, with emphasis put upon the great value of the minerals found there. The opinion given was that with adequate rail communication, the Okanogan country would be a second Comstock and would "rival any mineral-producing section thus far prospected within the confines of the Union."

The principal mines and claims on Ruby Hill and nearby in the Ruby district (with the dates of location) were: First Thought, Second Thought, Ruby (October, 1886), Fourth of July (April 1887), Arlington (May 1887), Butte (June 1886), Idaho (autumn, 1886), War Eagle, Lenora (September 1886), Peacock, Fairview, Poorman (October 1886). Jonathan Bourne Jr. (1855-1940), United States Senator from Oregon, and other Portland mining investors were interested in several of these mines. Average assays from the vein of the Fourth of July mine showed the ore to be worth over 100 dollars per ton.

However, this information presents pictures that are not easily reconciled. It appears that an actual lack of paying ore may have been the principal reason for the sluggish activity at the mines. As is often the case in a mining district, miners and prospectors find it easy to deceive themselves. The miner is the most hopefully optimistic of people. Such was the case in Ruby City. People were not finding the rich veins they expected. In spite of this, they continued to work the mines until a combination of forces caused the decline of the district.

Rubyites, in the strong belief of what the district had to offer, were not timid in imposing that belief on those who would listen. In reality, Ruby was only a small camp perched on the side of a mountain where mines were being worked with varying degrees of fervor and success. The bumptiousness so characteristic of the camp is plainly shown in the few remaining copies of the town's one newspaper, *The Ruby Miner*. An advertisement in the issue of June 2, 1892, which takes up some four out of the six columns of the four-page newspaper, asserts that:

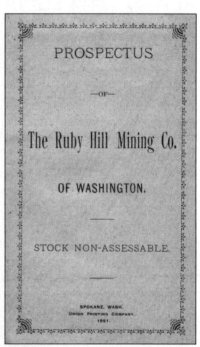

PROSPECTUS

—OF—

The Ruby Hill Mining Co.

OF WASHINGTON.

STOCK NON-ASSESSABLE.

SPOKANE, WASH.
UNION PRINTING COMPANY.
1891.

This rare and original financial report book Prospectus dates back to 1891. It was signed by O. Jeldness, Secretary of the Ruby Hill Mining Company, and was sent to all stockholders of said company.

"As Virginia City is to Nevada so is the town of Ruby to the State of Washington. Ruby is the only incorporated town in Okanogan

County. It is out of debt and has money in the Treasury. Public schools are open nine months every year, under the management of competent instructors, thus furnishing unsurpassed educational advantages. Let us make some money for you in Ruby. This district is appropriately termed the 'Comstock of Washington.' Nature has endowed Ruby with elements of a city. Man has supplied the adjuncts to make a metropolis."

Not only was the mining population concerned with the advent of more and more people into the town of Ruby, it planned to build another town close by. In the *Ellensburg Capital* for July 24, 1890, the following item appears:

"A new town has been laid out in the Okanogan country and named Leadville. Forces of men are now employed in clearing the brush and timber off the streets. It is located on a beautiful site about four miles below Ruby in the Salmon River Valley, through which the company will build their line of railroad to connect with the Washington Central at the Columbia River."

No accounts have been found to show that this second Leadville ever developed beyond the town site stage.

The youthful enthusiasm that characterized Ruby was not the only thing that drew people to the district. Curiosity also brought many visitors, and there is direct evidence that some of these were favorably impressed. Again in the *Ellensburg Capital* it is found that

"The prediction is freely made that it will equal if not exceed Leadville (Colorado). Mr. Ad Edgar, the veteran stage man, is also full of enthusiasm over the mines and predicts a glorious future for that region. He thinks that there will be one fine city and several splendid towns in that section and a wonderful influx will be witnessed as soon as the country is tapped by a railroad, which it now seems, will be the case inside of two years. When a railroad reaches the Okanogan, look out for a boom, so say all that have visited the mines."

Rubyites realized that transportation by freight wagon and light rig was not particularly helpful in developing the district. As the railroads extended their lines farther into the state, the promoters of Ruby made efforts to secure a branch line, which could run close to the mines. Time and time again throughout the newspaper articles of this period there is mention of railroads coupled with the belief that the day was not far distant when Ruby would receive rail service. That day never dawned for Ruby.

When it is realized that the Ruby district was not tapped by a railroad, the question arose concerning transportation into and out of the camp. For some time after the town was established, no regular means of transportation were in existence. Of course, freighters made trips to the various supply stations, Ellensburg being one of these. Its importance in this capacity came about in part because Ellensburg men did much to promote the town of Ruby and surrounding mines.

Ellensburg and Ruby were but four days apart by team and buggy. From Ruby, the trail dropped down the Salmon Creek to the Okanogan River at the Francis Jackson ("Pard") Cummings ranch, where the present town of Okanogan stands, or led over the Chiliwist, more to the southwest. The next stop was at the ferry to Foster Creek, where Bridgeport was located, across the Columbia River. From this ferry, the road led down the Columbia to Waterville. After dropping down through Corbelay Canyon, the Columbia was reached and recrossed where Orondo is now situated. Then the road ran down the west side of the river as far as Wenatchee. The last part of the journey was the crossing of Coluckum Pass and a ride into Ellensburg.

It is interesting to note just what made up the freight coming into the new country. According to a man who made a number of freighting trips to Ruby, sugar, flour, coffee, bacon, and syrup made up a large part of the provisions brought in. Other necessities were miners' tools, clothing, and liquor.

Spokane, Cheney, Sprague, and Coulee City, the terminus of the Central Washington Railroad, were also distribution centers. For a time, the higher grades of ore were freighted by team to Sprague, terminus of the Northern Pacific Railway, and shipped from there via Spokane to the Tacoma smelter. When the railroad reached Coulee City, the ore was hauled there and shipped to various smelting centers. Before the stage line was established in 1888, settlers at Ruby used to make up a purse to send a rider to Sprague for mail, at a charge of ten cents a letter. The stage road, the only means of communication with the outside world, ran from Coulee City, terminus of the Central Washington Railroad, to Penticton, British Columbia, at the foot of Okanogan Lake. It struck the south bank of the Columbia River at Foster Creek (Bridgeport), where the road divided. One branch crossed the Columbia there by ferry, traversed the southwest corner of the Indian reservation, and crossed the Okanogan River by ferry about seven miles above its mouth.

The other branch continued along the south bank of the Columbia and crossed the river by ferry at the river port of Virginia City. About ten miles above the mouth of the Okanogan, the two branches of the road reunited at Ophir. Near Alma, the road left the Okanogan and ran up the canyon of Salmon Creek to Ruby, thence six miles to Conconully. From Conconully, it ran over to and down the Sinlahekin and Similkameen, via Loomis, to Oroville, where it struck the Okanogan River again and ran north to Penticton

There were few good roads in the county. When mining districts were close enough together, the miners endeavored to build roads between camps. Such was the case between the towns of Ruby and Lomiston (Loomis). *The Ruby Miner* of March 2, 1892, made a plea for the completion of a road between these two towns. Most of the road, apparently, had been built. *The Ruby Miner* contended that "this leaves a gap of only about three miles to build, and if the citizens of Ruby will raise 300 dollars in either money or labor, this piece of road can be completed in 30 days." Here again is noted that sluggishness which was mentioned earlier.

Three hundred dollars is not a large amount to raise in a thriving mining town, but it was in Ruby. The paper concluded its plea by asserting that "by the middle of

Looking down Main Street Ruby, where over a century ago it was known as the Queen City of the Okanogan County mining boom. Today, the town site is in a lonely, forested canyon a few miles northwest of the town of Okanogan.

April (we) should have one of the best roads in Okanogan County, between its two principal towns."

In summing up the story of transportation in the Ruby mining district, it can be said that the first roads were merely trails through the tall bunch grass. These trails later developed into well-traveled roads, which may or may not have followed closely the original trails. Efforts were made to build roads from the steamer landings on the Columbia to the mines, between the mining districts, and within a particular district. The Ruby mining district and the others surrounding it never had satisfactory roads.

Guy Waring gives one of the better descriptions of Ruby: "Ruby, in 1888, was at the height of its power. Miners and prospectors were flowing there from all over the Northwest, and more than a thousand men and women inhabited the town, which lay for a quarter of a mile along a single graded street, built up solidly on either side with stores and mostly log houses. Available photographs show a predominance of frame buildings in the camp, rather than those of the log-cabin type."

Visitors in the town did not always find the accommodations desirable. On the occasion one of his trips to Ruby, Austin Mires related in his diary:

> "We slept in the store where our old friend George Hurley was clerk-ing, making our beds down on the floor in the deep dust. Only a portion of the store had been provided with flooring and on the ground part, along near the center, the dust was from two to three inches deep. At this time, Ruby was one of the dustiest places I ever saw. Tents and buildings were without floors, and there were no sidewalks."

The town had a number of hotels. Waring recounted that there were no sheets upon the bed of a hotel where he once stayed. He spent a night there to be rewarded

A rare historic stock certificate from the Ruby Hill Mining Company dated March 1891.

with experiences decidedly foreign to him. He said, "I had placed my revolver under my pillow where I could reach it in an emergency, for Ruby provided any number of emergencies daily and nightly throughout the year, and I was prepared for most anything." Nor was his preparation in vain.

Around midnight, he awoke to discover a man snoring on the floor near his cot. The man was furious when awakened and asked to get out. He told Waring that he had paid for sleeping space in the hotel. Waring related: "Of course I had never before slept in a Ruby hotel and knowing nothing about the customs, I could not be sure that the man was not justified in being angry." He apologized to the other occupant. In the morning, he questioned the hotelkeeper. To his surprise, he found that the man knew nothing about it. The only solution to the enigma was that a drunken miner had gone up the stairs during the night and selected Waring's room as most convenient. Another visit in Ruby found Waring seeking quarters in George Hurley's store.

> "The owner received me kindly, and when I explained that I had no desire to put up at any of the town's so called hotels, he offered at once to let me sleep in the store. As usual, he told me to take down from the shelves as many blankets as I might need for my comfort and to make my bed on the counter."

Besides its importance as the center of a mining district, Ruby had another claim to fame. It was the first county seat of Okanogan County. Until 1888, the Okanogan country was a part of Stevens County. The territorial legislature in that year enacted a measure creating Okanogan County and naming three temporary county commissioners to organize the new county, appoint its first officers, and to select a temporary county seat. Residents of Ruby decided that their town should be the county seat, while citizens of Salmon City (Conconully) planned likewise for their town. The three county commissioners held their first meeting at the John Perkins ranch on Johnson Creek, four miles north of Ruby, as directed by the law. Guy Waring, one of the commissioners, has left a realistic description of the meeting, March 6, 1888:

> "It was an occasion I shall never forget. The people of Ruby, hearing of the meeting, all turned out to hold a noisy celebration in our honor. Whores, thieves, and drunkards, and other notorious citizens of the mining town were on hand some time before the oath of office was administered. They were of course agreeably drunk, and serenaded us so loudly that it was difficult for anybody inside the ranch house to hear himself speak."

Petitions and spokesman from Ruby and Salmon City were received. Much to Waring's disgust, Ruby was voted the county seat. It was not necessary to erect many new buildings to house county business, for all the county officers occupied one little shack. Since the county had no safe-deposit vault, when the treasurer had on hand about 1,800 dollars in cash, he put it into an empty baking powder can and buried it on his ranch

The selection of county officers and the location of a county seat by the commissioners were both temporary arrangements. The first county officers were to serve until March 1889 or until their successors were elected and qualified. The county seat was to be permanently located by a choice of the qualified voters at the next general election (November 6, 1888), when they should also elect their county officers. In a diary written by Benedict Gubser of Conconully is the following entry: "October 30, 1888. Went to Ruby. Took a deer ham along but had a hard time selling it. Ruby people did not believe in patronizing Conconully people. The county seat question was at white heat." Rubyites were not successful in their second attempt to secure the county seat, for Conconully received 357 votes and Ruby but 157. The county officers were removed to Conconully in February 1889.

Few records remain concerning government in Ruby previous to the time it became the temporary county seat. Like other camps, it had the officials necessary to carry on mining with some degree of legality, such as miner's recorders and judges. According to Waring, the law did not go much further than that. He himself served as justice of the peace in his own section of the Okanogan country, and admitted that his job would have been more difficult had he served in that capacity in Ruby or Conconully. In part, he said:

> "Among the mining population every conceivable crime, except interfering with virtuous women, took place at least once in the course of a year, and in Ruby even more frequently. Killings among the miners were very common, and both whites and Siwashes had a hand in them. But the worst of it was, nothing ever happened to the guilty parties. Either they bribed the justices or escaped from the territory."

Ruby grew up too quickly and died out to suddenly for the historian to get an accurate picture of every phase of life there. Records have been left, however, that tell something of the social life. There were several ways in which the population found diversion. One of these was hunting in the surrounding country. In the diary of Benedict Gubser is an account of a visit with a certain Andy Funk. This man related to Gubser that he killed 96 deer that season (1888) in order to break the record of one "Sago," who had killed 92. In the diary of Austin Mires is an account of a hunting trip in the Ruby country during which he and his companions "ran onto tracks of more than 50 deer that had passed along in the early morning."

Dances were seemingly all-inclusive as a means of entertainment. E.C. Sherman, first treasurer of Okanogan County, has given an excellent description of them. He was of the opinion that Ruby was one of the most sociable resorts for miners and prospectors to be found in any mining region. Quite often, the honorable board of (county) commissioners called a half-hour recess and conferred on some pressing question that was unfathomable anywhere except at one of the refreshment foot rails. In those days, dried or jerked venison was plentiful, and miners spent sociable evenings drinking the brewery lager beer of Ruby, chewing dried venison and singing.

The people of Conconully, Ruby, and the ranches for miles around were like one big family when it came to amusements. All were acquainted. The women brought sandwiches, cake, and coffee to dances and entertainments. The babies and children slept on benches or boxes. Strangers were introduced to whole gatherings at one moment, and the dance went on merrily.

Another means of spending leisure time was the saloon. Just how many saloons Ruby had in its heyday is a figure open to question. Opinion ranks them in number from six to 20. Activity at the close of day can well be imagined as prospectors, miners, and cowboys poured into the town. "Ruby was wide open and often there were thousands of dollars in sight on the gaming tables."

There were also present in Ruby that undesirable social aspect so common to mining towns. Waring gives an almost too realistic picture of this phase in relation to other forces, particularly the law.

> "On this particular afternoon (in March 1888), the town was in the heat of excitement over the latest of its many notorious murders, which, as I soon learned, had occurred early that same morning. It seems that one of Ruby's more lecherous citizens had attempted shortly before dawn to gain admittance to the town's chief brothel house in a state of complete intoxication. When the mistress of the house, greatly annoyed at being diverted from her business at such an hour, refused to permit him to enter, the gentleman, according to the report I gathered, took a swing at her. Thereupon the mistress, not to miss having the last word on the doorstep of her own establishment, returned to her room for a revolver and shot the gentleman through the heart, killing him instantly.
>
> "His body had been found crumpled upon the steps outside the house, and by the time the sheriff could be persuaded to inquire at the establishment for details of the "accident" the mistress had found time to board the stage for Spokane Falls. She knew, of course, that a few days later the whole affair would be forgotten in the interest of some new scandal in the town, and she could return unmolested by the law to her former mode of living. As I listened to a group of citizens expound the merits of the case, I gained a still better idea of the level of morality one could expect to find in Ruby. No one cared much about the actual facts of the murder. The chief point of dispute was whether or not the madam had taken a previous dislike to her unwelcome client because of the damage he had done to her staff of girls. For it was generally known in Ruby, I learned, that the gentleman's much-discussed limp had been caused by neither infantile paralysis, rheumatism, nor any other common form of affliction or accident.
>
> "When I had heard all I wanted to about the deceased and his scandalous limp, I went on to the county auditor's office. There I was forced to listen to a further version of the murder by an official,

who, as he casually explained, had been inside the brothel at the time of the shooting and stumbled over the dead body on his way out in the morning."

Waring had difficulties with various members of the populace. Perhaps he felt a bitterness that made him enlarge upon an account of this nature. On the other hand, the Ruby town council instructed the marshal in 1892 to remove all houses of ill fame off the Main Street.

Virginia Grainger as county superintendent. (Photo from State Superintendent of Public Instruction, Olympia.)

The character of social life in Ruby goes far to explain education and religion in the camp. There is some information concerning education, beginning about 1890. Although the camp had one of the earlier schools in the county, there was but a small number of children of school age in Ruby. It was in 1890 that Mrs. Virginia Grainger took over her duties as fifth county superintendent of education. One of the greatest difficulties of her term arose over the erection of a school at Ruby. According to her, there were about 30 prospective pupils in District 3; slightly more than half that number would be in regular attendance. Some of the most active residents, with the backing of a large floating population, wanted to bond the school district for 5,000 dollars and build a schoolhouse large enough to be used also as a community hall. Mrs. Grainger refused to sign either the bonds or the contract for the erection of the building. The work went ahead, however, without her signature.

Her opponents bitterly resented the views she held, and the point was brought up that a woman was not eligible to hold that office. While she refused to turn her books over to the county commissioners. When completed, the school was used as had been planned. Mrs. Grainger taught in this school for a year. Arriving there one morning, she discovered four pupils, from five to 11 years of age, lying drunk near the school. A dance had been held the previous evening, and the contents of the bottles left lying about were sufficient to cause intoxication. About the only conclusion one can draw from the last part of this episode is that liquor must indeed have flowed freely in Ruby.

Religion, like education, seems to have played a minor part in the life of the camp prior to 1890. After that year the evidence offered throws no direct light on the town itself, but rather on the surrounding communities. On February 8, 1891, Benedict Gubser entered in his diary:

"A Presbyterian minister named Anderson preached in town (Conconully) tonight."

Under the date of August 14, 1893, Gubser wrote:

"A young Presbyterian minister gave me a short call today. He is stationed at Lomiston (Loomis) until the last of next month, when he intends to return to college. He preaches in half a dozen places. He belongs over the line, but does nearly all his work on this side. He says his best congregation is at Carpenter's about 10 miles below Ruby."

Like many other frontier camps, Ruby figured in an Indian uprising. This occurred in January 1891 and had its beginning in the murder of S.S. Cole, a freighter. One of the alleged Indian murderers was killed in a gun battle by a deputy sheriff. The second Indian, named Stephen, was lodged in the jail at Conconully. A lynching party broke into the jail, secured Stephen, and hanged him. The Indian scare followed this incident. What was really done to anger the Indians is a phase of the story that has never been clear. People present in the Okanogan country at the time of the uprising believed in later years that the hostile attitude of the Indians was overestimated and that it amounted to a "feverish dream" among the whites.

According to one source, the Okanogan braves were angered because the man who transported the body of Stephen from Conconully to a Catholic cemetery at St. Mary's Mission sat on the coffin, which was carried on a bobsled. The settlers believed the Indians were preparing for war and asked acting Governor Charles E. Laughton for troops. "The women and children were gathered together by night and taken to Ruby, where it was planned to barricade them in the Fourth of July mine in case of necessity." A conference was held with the Indians, however, and further trouble was averted.

As has been indicated, the early '90s saw the beginning of the decline of Ruby. A number of reasons may be given for this, chief among them the fall in the price of silver. No doubt this factor served to bring to a head the final doom of the camp. Ruby dwindled rapidly from a once-prosperous mining town of several hundred inhabitants to a mere several dozen by the autumn of 1894. There was still a store, a hotel, a fine school building, and about a hundred dwelling houses. The mines on Ruby Hill, however, worked for three months in 1893, were shut down after the fall in silver prices.

Viewed in the perspective of 114 years, one of the main reasons for the decline of Ruby seems to have been a definite lack of high-grade ore, regardless of the price of silver. Hope was continually expressed that before long the district would become one of the richest of its kind, but that hope never fulfilled. That which bred the camp was to cause its destruction. The plea for a railroad was never answered, nor were local road connections ever built as to permit speedy transportation. These three things, then, the fall in the price of silver, the absence of a sufficient amount of paying ore, and the lack of cheap transportation, were the main factors in the destruction of Ruby.

That the business enterprises of the town early suffered as a result of the decline in mining may be witnessed by an article in the *Conconully Okanogan Outlook*, April 29, 1892:

The Panic of 1893, a national depression, and the Silver Purchase Act of 1890 forced the government to stop buying silver. The mining boom collapsed overnight; work ceased; and mining camps were abandoned. (Photo from Okanogan County Historical Society collection).

"*The Ruby Miner* has resumed publication again under the new management. F.J. Long, formerly employed in the mechanical department of the paper, has taken the helm and will try to steer its course so as to avoid the shoals and breakers so frequently encountered on the sea of journalism. We wish him every success in his undertaking."

The life of the *Ruby Miner* under its new leadership must have been very short indeed.

There is an incident concerning Ruby that is more legendary than factual. True or not, it has added color to the story of the town and for that is written down here. A certain miner had been "rolled" and robbed in Ruby. He is said to have stationed himself on a hill overlooking the town and to have cursed it so all could hear. "May you be burned, drowned, and burned again." If this story is true and has not suffered the distortions of time, it is rather interesting in the light of the events that followed.

In 1894, the floodwaters that washed away a portion of the town of Conconully came down Salmon Creek to Ruby. The people had been warned, however, and everyone got to a point of safety. The damage done to the town was not extensive, and only a few houses were washed away. Most important of all (in the minds of the more thirsty Rubyites) was the fact that the brewery was damaged by the floodwater.

From the time of the flood until 1900, there are few records of happenings in Ruby. It is known that each succeeding year found fewer and fewer people there.

Some of the miners sought other fields; many of them went north into British Columbia. Others started farming in nearby vicinities. Business and professional men sought other towns.

The spirit that Ruby had known in the days of its greatest activity must have stayed alive through its waning years. When only three inhabitants were left, it is related that a city government was sustained. Austin Mires passed through Ruby in 1898. Years later, he told newspapermen of the trip. Part of his story is quoted here.

> "At this time, 1898, as we passed through Ruby it held just three inhabitants—Ned Paine and two other parties. One was called the hotelkeeper, and the other had the livery stable. They were holding down the city government. Paine was mayor, one of the others was the city clerk and the other, marshal. On August 28, 1899, I passed through Ruby again with my family on our way to Republic and the town was entirely deserted. The buildings were all in tact (sic), but there was not a single inhabitant."

In all probability, the town did not remain intact for long. Ranchers in the vicinity tore down and hauled away many of the buildings. About 1900, fire aided the destruction that had already taken place. By 1904, only a "few buildings, riddled and tottering," still stood, "monuments" to mark the spot where once this boomtown stood.

Now in 2001, the "monuments" which the historian saw in 1904 are gone. Before many more years have passed, there will be no trace of the camp that Guy Waring called "the Babylon of the West." Today, even the ghosts have departed.

OLD LOUP LOUP:
THE LOST CITY

Here on the floor of the dense forest are the unmistakable prints of the lost city, Old Loup Loup, the first platted town in Okanogan County. Still distinct in the shadowy light are foundations indicating buildings up to 60 feet in length that once lined the wide main streets known as Conconully, Okanogan, Methow, Nespelem, and Wenatchee. Bricks from crumpled chimneys lie exposed in spots, although the forest began covering up signs of the little city that once blazed in the glory of a new mining epoch over 113 years ago.

Loup Loup was the rival sister of Ruby City and lay about four miles over Ruby Hill from her. It was platted in the Loup Loup Valley on August 14, 1888, by W.P. Keady and S.F. Chadwick. Little is known about Keady, but Chadwick was ex-governor of Oregon and the father of Stephen J. Chadwick, a member of the Supreme Court of Washington.

According to Phillip H. Pinkston, who came to Okanogan County in 1888 to act as agent for the owners of the Loup Loup town site, 80 acres of script was filed on the site, and a boomtown began exploding.

The platt shows that the two main streets, Okanogan and Methow, were 80 feet wide. The other streets, Wenatchee and Conconully, narrowed toward the city edges. Lots were 25x90 feet and sold at $200 to $500 each.

To get mining supplies and equipment into Loup Loup, the promoters scratched a road from Malott through Pleasant Valley and the Buzzard Lake section.

Pinkston was notified to put up a gate and place a man on the road to collect tolls, but insufficient travel caused that plan to fall through. An effort was then made to sell the road to the county, but that venture also failed.

By 1890, the mining town had enough people to warrant the establishment of a post office. On January 18 of that year, Phillip H. Pinkston became the official postmaster. The office was established under the name of Loop. Whether this was a recording error or not is not known, but on June 30 of that same year it was changed to Loup Loup.

Pinkston was a man of vision, and according to an old newspaper record, he filed a water right on the west fork of the Salmon Creek and had a route surveyed for a ditch to bring water for power and domestic use to both Ruby and Loup Loup.

Pinkston said that at the height of its boom, Loup Loup had a population of 400 people. Mrs. John (Annie) Hilderbrand, a resident of Loup Loup, also estimated this number.

It was March 29, 1890, when newlyweds Mr. and Mrs. John Hilderbrand arrived in the little mining city. Loup Loup was at that time engulfed in deep snowdrifts following a harsh winter. Barnyard fences all across the Big Bend and through the Okanogan, she noted, were hung with cowhides that indicated the heavy loss of stock due to the severe winter.

Annie Hilderbrand said there were from 30 to 40 dwelling houses in Loup Loup during the time they lived there. The town had a boarding house, a building for mining supplies, a general store, a post office, a meat market, and several other establishments. Bacom's Lumber Mill was nearby.

Hilderbrand bought horses and was soon employed by Jonathan Bourne, who hailed from the First Thought Mine, where a crew of 100 or more men was employed. One of the loads of precious ore was considered so valuable that an escort of men with loaded rifles guarded it out of the area.

In 1892, Bourne had a concentrator built at Ruby, and it was connected with the mine by a cable tramway that carried the ore over the Ruby Hill in buckets and dumped it into ore bins above the concentrator for processing.

The Hilderbrands lived in the north end of Loup Loup. That section was called Fundlerville, as Fundler, a man who operated the War Eagle and other mines on Peacock lived there.

In 1893, the price of silver dropped, and the glow began to fade from the mines. The Hilderbrands moved to Ruby, but it, too, was gasping for breath. However, the Loup Loup post office continued to operate until November 20, 1895, when it was discontinued and mail transferred to Ruby.

And so a city died. Frame houses were moved away, and the forest crept over the site. Only one or two persons really know of its location today. Most people passing have no idea a mining town once flourished there.

Could this perhaps be the site of The Lost City?

THE OLD TOWN OF NIGHTHAWK

There are a lot of things about this area that are not really even known by the people that live here, such as the fact that U.S. Mineral Monument #1 is located close by. The land I own once belonged to "Okanogan" Smith. He patented this land in 1883. The mines I own and many others in the area were the first ones registered in the Territory of Washington. Most of the documentation and information I have in my possession I found digging through land records and mining claims at the courthouse.

The Nighthawk Hotel was built by J.M. Hagerty in 1903, partially burned down in 1910, and was rebuilt shortly thereafter. Most boomtowns in those days had a house of ill repute, and Nighthawk was no exception. The building located behind the cathouse (as it was called) was known as the old Doc. Andrus livery stable.

The main street in Nighthawk was Prospect Avenue. It is still referred by this name today, but without the horses, wagons, and miners. The schoolhouse, which also still stands today on private land, was built sometime around 1915 and was the place where many pioneer children in the area received their education.

The Kaaba Texas Mine is one of the best preserved mines in Okanogan County with many of the original buildings still standing today. The small building was the

The Kaaba Texas concentration mill built around 1939 remains today with its massive original crushing equipment intact. This mill is said to be one of the best-preserved mills in Okanogan County.

main office. The large wedge-shaped building was the old mill building, where the ores were processed from the mine. The assay office that once stood with these remaining structures burned down many years ago.

There were settlers here as early as 1862, but it was just a tent town and died out around 1870. It is said that there were as many as 3,000 men living here by 1865.

Nighthawk was to become a recognized town on Nov. 18, 1903. It was platted by the Nighthawk Realty Co. and owned by Myron J. Church and Chas T. Peterson and was accepted by the Land Office in Waterville, Washington on Feb. 16, 1904. The rail came through about 1905 and the train depot store was built on May 6, 1906.

NIGHTHAWK MINING CLAIMS TURN TO RICHES

The Nighthawk District has many of the oldest claims, including the first registered hard-rock claims in the state of Washington. In a journal entry by J.M. Haggerty, the man that took over Hiram F. "Okanogan" Smith's mining property after Smith's death in 1893, writes: "That by 1865 there were some 3,000 miners that flocked to a spot on the Similkameen River known as Rich Bar. In his writings, he says that "Okanogan" Smith, acting as agent for Wells Fargo & Company, ships $600,000 in the first 60 days of the rush from Rich Bar, all taken from a stretch not exceeding four acres in extent."

It's unknown how much gold was really taken from the Similkameen River. The entire river was rich with deposits. Even today, one can go to the river and pan, get lucky, and find gold flakes and black sand, and come home with a nice large gold nugget. The gold rush on the Similkameen was brought to a halt when the river suddenly rose and washed out all wing dams built by miners. Tales of gold in places like Rock Creek, Trail Creek, and the city of Roseland lured miners to what they hoped would be richer, easier bonanza finds than that of Similkameen River.

Photo on the left: Hiram F. "Okanogan" Smith farmed near Oroville. He planted the first orchard, filed the first mining claim, served in the state legislature, and otherwise distinguished himself as a pioneering citizen. (Photo from Okanogan County Historical Society collection). Photo on the right: Remnants of an abandoned miner's cabin on Mount Chopaka near Ruby Mill.

At the time, no one paid much attention to large outcroppings of quartz vein material that was scattered around Little Chopaka Mountain. "Okanogan" Smith kept his eye on them, however, and in April 1873, Mr. Smith and a few friends made the first locations in the territory of Washington.

It was too far to ship the ore, and President Hayes, by presidential proclamation, made everything north and west of the Columbia River an Indian reservation. It was not until 1883, after exhaustive work by Mr. Smith and others, that President Hayes opened everything north and west of the Columbia River (which became known as the 15-mile strip) for mining claims. The mines still could not be worked, however, as they were enclosed by the Indian reservation for 100 miles around it.

In 1886, the rest of the north half of the Moses Reservation was opened to claiming, and the rush was on. Mines began to pop up all over the country. The biggest producing mines in the Nighthawk District were Four Metals, Cabba, Nighthawk, Six Eagles, Number One, Summit Silver, Wyandotte, Peerless, Chopaka, Ruby Silver Mine, Golden Zone, and Mt. Sheep Mine.

US Mineral Monument # 1 was established on the Summit Silver claim, as the Nighthawk District had not been surveyed as to township, ranges, or sections at that time. Many of these mines had their own concentration mills, which supported a refinery about five miles north east of Nighthawk. There were at least six concentration mills in this area, all operating at the same time. For various reasons, the mines and mills closed down, mainly due to the drop in demand of precious metals. The last mill to shut down was the Kabba Texas Mine in 1951.

The Ruby Silver Mine was the most famous of them all. The Ruby was 950 feet in the main adit; there are some 5,000 feet of drifts and raises. It was located in April 1902 by A.M. Riste and George Bowers, and was sold on November 15, 1902 to the Ruby Mining Company, which at this time J.M. Haggerty took over as the main boss of operation. In January 1903, work began to develop the ore body, and in the first year of development it produced over $20,000 in silver values in 211 feet of adit. It also blocked out another 20,000 tons of ore that averaged $50.00 a ton. This mine is one of the very few mines anywhere that paid for its development work with

Deserted Ruby Mine Mill stands today on private land north of Loomis.

money left over. It has been said the mine received its name from the fact that the silver ore under miners' carbide lamps would make the ore appear ruby red in color. The Ruby Mine was worked into the 1960s off and on.

Not all the mines are closed down completely, but none are producing ore at this time. There are diamond drill programs running at Four Metals, and the Nighthawk Mine is still being sampled. There has been work done at the Ruby Mine, with the hope that one day the price of silver will make it profitable to work these mines once again. Ruby Mine is on private property and is posted as such, but can be viewed from the road. Mines and mine shafts are DANGEROUS. Please respect the No Trespassing signs.

Okanogan County was not about to surrender her riches easily. The bonanza boom was built on laborious efforts to tap mother loads secreted in massive formations of rock. Old bonanza mine portal entrance near Nighthawk.

Hart's Pass Area History

Kjell Lester is the proprietor of the White Buck Trading Company in Winthrop, Washington. This story was told to him by his grandfather, Bill Lester, and Dick Horn, both of whom spent time working in the Hart's Pass area in the 1920s and 1930s.

The Hart's Pass area in 1895 was a booming gold mining town. During the peak working era, there were 3,500 people working and living at the mines.

There were three hotels, a general store, a post office, a blacksmith shop, a sawmill, a power plant, and a saloon.

At Chancellor, a power plant was built in hopes that a railroad would eventually meet up with it. The power plant ran lines throughout the area and generated lights, and the electricity was a DC current run by water going through a Pelton wheel. They used DC because the technology wasn't refined for AC and DC was much easier to work with. The hopes of huge deposits of gold and posterity diminished, however, and the thoughts of a railroad were eventually forgotten.

The blacksmith shop was one of the busiest places in camp and could be compared today to a machinist—he would fix anything that broke down. He forged tools and sharpened the chisel-bitted steel that was used deep in the mines for making blasting holes.

The general store had clothes for the miners as well as groceries or anything else they might need. At the Bonita Mine (now known as the Western Gold), there was a butcher shop with fresh meat.

The sawmills were constructed to cut rough lumber to build all the buildings that so many people demanded. Lots of the buildings were made from logs on the outside, with the rough lumber used on the inside, and these sawmills were used several years later for the same purpose. The sawmills were run by water wheels, one of which is now is on display at the Shafer Museum in Winthrop.

One of the hotels had rooms in the upper stories, and the post office located on the bottom floor. The saloon was the entertainment for the evenings and employed ladies to dance with the men and sit with them.

A Saturday in the life of one of those miners might go something like this: Awakening at dawn, he gets up and trudges up to the mine after fixing himself a hot breakfast. He is helping dig a tunnel deep in the mountain to follow the ore vein. He gets off a couple hours early because it's Saturday. It's a nice hot day, so there is a slim chance he might take a bath before he goes to the saloon, but he might not, too. Down at the saloon, he goes to dance, drink, and share stories with other miners. He'd go home around midnight so he could get up early to work the next day in the mines.

The road to Hart's Pass was a narrow gauge wagon road, so miners would cut down wagons to make them narrower so they could carry supplies by wagons to the mine. Horses were used in pack strings. In the 1890s, a pack string was headed in with supplies, and in a very narrow stretch of road that had planks over it, one of the last horses pulled back, not wanting to cross. Since the horses were all tied together, the other horses lost their footing, and the whole string went off the edge of the road, falling several hundred feet to the bottom of Rattlesnake Creek. This narrow stretch of road that still exists today is now called Dead Horse Point.

Some of the mines produced lots of gold. The Bonita Mine, for example, gave up $250,000 in one pocket. The Glory Hole was right above the Bonita and had gold right on the surface; these were called "float" veins. The Mammoth Mine was located near the saloon, and part of the saloon building still stands today.

Bill Lester, Kjell's grandfather, worked for the Forest Service and started making treks into the Hart's Pass area in 1924. In 1926, he walked through one of the hotels that was vacant, picked up a mattress on one of the beds, and found an older version of a $1.00 bill. In 1930, Dick Horn went into the post office, and letters were lying all over the floor and counters—when people abandoned the area, they didn't even bring the mail out to be forwarded. Food like macaroni and flour were still in the bins at the grocery store.

In 1930, Dick Horn came to Winthrop from Spokane as a young man. He helped widen the Hart's Pass narrow gauge road in places. He worked for Charlie Ballard, who was the president of the stockholders of the Azurite Mine. The road still was not wide enough for a regular car to travel on it. Charlie Ballard had bought a few Fords and cut 10 inches off the axles to make them narrow enough to drive to and from the mine. To freight large amounts, a 15-horsepower caterpillar tractor hauled the supplies. The cat had special cleats for the wintertime.

Charlie Ballard and stockholders ran the mine from 1930 to 1934. They built the Tinson Tunnel to intercept the vein that ran from the surface at the top of the mountain. The Tinson Tunnel was about 500 feet deep. Six hundred feet below the Tinson, a second tunnel was built and called the Wenatchee. This tunnel was 1,200 feet deep. The vein went up at a 60-degree angle, and a skip bucket on a cable and wench helped carry the miners up to the vein because it was so steep. At the top, where the vein was, it measured 68 feet wide, and the ore assayed at $60 a ton. From the Discovery Hole to the Wenatchee Tunnel was approximately 800 feet, so that's how deep the vein was. Gold was $35 an ounce at that time.

To process this ore, a Mace Smelter was built. It was capable of processing 30 tons of ore every 24 hours, which was considered fairly small. Dick Horn helped build a $\frac{3}{4}$-mile road to a quarry from the Azurite Mine.

Here's a sample of how the smelter would have worked:

A couple of shovels full of ore were put in the fire, then a shovel full of coke, lime, and quartz. The coke created heat; a blower circulated the air, and the heat melted the ore until it ran like milk. Then it was poured into steel and firebrick-lined crucible (ore car). There were two spouts on the side of the car, one 8 inches above the other. A clay plug on a crowbar was hammered into the car, and the ore would come out the holes. The lower hole is where the valuable "matt" would come out. The higher hole is where the non-valuable "slag" came out. They were both put in molds, left to cool, and then dumped out of the molds. The slag was normally dumped over the hill, where it still lies today, and the matt was hauled by a caterpillar to Robinson Creek then trucked to Pateros and put on a railroad car to the Tacoma Smelter. The assay of the matt was worth $300 a ton.

Dick Horn was foreman of the Azurite Mine from 1932 to 1933. In 1934, the mine was leased to the American Smelting and Refining Company. At that time, the vein was 68 feet wide. As they went lower, the vein suddenly narrowed; it would vary from 2 feet to 4 feet wide. Because of that, in 1938, the American Smelting closed down production. When American Smelting left, they tore the mill down and brought out most of the material that was used to build the mill. Today, it's too expensive to build another mill to process any gold that might still remain there.

In 1930 to 1932, Dick Horn carried the mail into the Azurite Mine in winter. His main place to stay was the cabin at Robinson Creek, which has since burned down. On a typical day, Dick would snowshoe nine miles south to Mazama and pick up the mail for the approximately 5 to 10 men working at the mine. He would then go back to his cabin to spend the night. Next morning he would snowshoe 24 miles north to the Azurite. If the weather was bad, he'd get 12 miles and stay at the cabin at Horse Heaven and go the other 12 miles the next day. He usually made it out in one day. He would repeat this every 10 days, unless there was an emergency that he needed to get word to someone sooner. Dick was the only link to civilization for these men in the winter.

Dick Horn was caught in a snowslide in 1931 and was carried $\frac{1}{4}$ of a mile. He was buried up to his shoulder on one side and to his armpit on the other. Dick ended up with broken ribs and a sprained ankle. He was black and blue all over his stomach and down his lower leg and foot. One of his snowshoes was broken, but he managed to hike the three miles to the mine. He was sure that if he hadn't had a strong will to live, he could have easily given up and died.

In 1935, the road to Hart's Pass was finally widened enough to have a normal car travel it, and then the ore and gold was freighted out by trucks.

Today, there are some mines that are being worked in the summer months, such as the Brown Bear Mine, which is at the top of Hart's Pass. The Western Gold is still producing. Today, people use new portable dredges in the streams.

The road is being studied to decide whether to close it or improve it for others to use. It would be terrible to close this history of the past to people. The only way we can learn what our pioneer ancestors did and where they went is to see this history firsthand.

INFORMATION ON METAL DETECTING AND RELIC HUNTING

COLLECTING WASHINGTON'S BOOM TOWNS

Over the past several years, more and more people are discovering the pleasure and challenges of "collecting" ghost towns. There are ghost towns in every state, but some of the most picturesque and intriguing of all ghost towns are to be found in the mountains, foothills, and valleys of Northeastern Washington State. Collecting Northeastern Washington ghost towns is a tough job, because this part of our Evergreen State was the heart of mining and boomtowns that once housed thousands of miners and settlers. Now, they are uninhabited and in many cases, a challenge to locate.

Historic abandoned mining ghost town.

There are many reasons for "collecting" ghost towns. The reasons vary with individuals and places, and the variations seem endless. The binding similarity of all the reasons, however, is the sense of adventure to be had in seeking out lost and forgotten boomtowns of yesteryear. Simply finding such spots is enough to drive some ghost towners wild with excitement. Such people love to hear of a new ghost town site, research its location, seek out this relic from the past, and add it to their "collection" of sites visited. Photography leads some into hunting for lost ghost towns, as does hiking and being in touch with nature.

Many of the sites are in beautiful locations enhanced by decaying, ramshackle ruins. Avid history buffs can easily fall prey to the habit of seeking out ghost towns.

It is fortunate that most of the avid ghost town seekers value the sites highly and scrupulously leave the sites as they found them. It is unfortunate that others also come to ghost towns—many just to vandalize such unprotected places.

It is good that ghost towns attract the attention of interested history buffs, for as all man-made things, the ghost towns do not last forever. Nature destroys such places completely. Winds tear things loose and blow them every which way. Deep snows pile high on roofs already weak with dry rot and sagging from many former snows. Weak, they yield to strains and fall. When the roofs go, the walls do not stand long, and in a few short years there is only a rotting pile of wood. Even that rots back into the earth, new growth hiding the displaced earth of foundations. The relentless truth of nature, with large and small bites, gnaws endlessly at the abandoned works of man, and the wilds reclaim their own.

The ghost town site, emptied of almost all evidence of its boomtown existence, is becoming the most common kind of ghost town in Northeastern Washington. A few cellar pits, portions of retaining walls, a few hints of raised stone foundations, and, as one looks closer, endless bits of scattered glass and metal tins are the remains of better times.

Today's ghost town collector needs to be more interested in the site than in the town itself. Such a person's imagination must put flesh back on the scattered wooden skeletal remains. To the history buff that can do this, the ghost town sites come back to life, ghosts of miners and buildings rebuilt in the visitor's mind's eye.

If collecting ghost towns sounds like fun, try it. Come to historic Northeastern Washington State and seek among the foothills, mountains, and valleys for remains of ghost towns long ago forgotten.

Getting the Relics out of Bare Bones Ghost Towns

Many a site of former glory is bypassed these days even by treasure hunters. Ignored, unknown, forgotten, once-thriving boomtowns have literally bit the dust from one end of this country to the other. Not much remains to show the activity that formerly went on in such places. Rare coins lost from those places of business and areas where folks congregated, however, the artifacts lost or cast aside, and now

This rare historic Derby's saloon token was excavated at an old mine site near Twisp, Washington. This is the only specific known historic Derby's saloon token to be in existence today.

valuable odds and ends, rest hidden and undisturbed beneath the dust and over-growth. These are the bare bones of dead ghost towns. Upon these long ago lost sites, you seekers of treasure, there are still many relics.

Rare coins, trade tokens, saloon tokens, tools, and all sorts of worthwhile relics remain, right where they fell or were placed, in the remnants of boomtowns long dead. Why does a town die? Mining towns die when the ores play out or the price of silver drops. Other towns even die before this if a new town in a better location springs up nearby. Ore deposits do not last forever. Gold, silver, copper, or anything else wrenched from the protective earth is of measurable limits.

A rare and original post card the author obtained from a collector, with the famous Derby's saloon in the background. Sign being held reads: "Halloween Dance and Carnival Winthrop Oct. 27 by Winthrop Band." Also, front of large building in background reads "Twisp Department Store."

If a town's sole support is the output of a mine, the town is doomed to ultimate desertion. Only some new industry, farming, agriculture, cattle, or lumber can save it. When the resource is exhausted, the wages stop, people begin to leave, and the town dies. In time, nature quietly and completely reclaims its own.

One thing to remember as a ghost town treasure hunter is that simply because a town dies, no matter what the reason, if it was really a going boomtown, the site is well worth looking over. Things were left, things were lost, and those relics from yes-teryear are just waiting to be found.

There are some common-sense dos and don'ts in hunting ghost towns. No mat-ter where you hunt, have permission if it's required, or know it is not required. If it is on private property, don't fail to get permission before you begin your search. If permission is not possible, don't hunt it. As confusing as they are, attempt to know your state laws concerning treasure hunting and the status of ghost towns in your state. Some states really don't have any such laws.

Don't leave holes. Fill in everything you dig. If you have to disrupt some sod, do your best to put the clump back so as not to retard its survival. Don't vandalize.

Remember, do your research, find the old ghost town sites, and search them. The coins, tokens, jewelry, and relics from yesteryear are still there. Good luck!

The Challenges of Metal Detecting Boom Towns

It should be understood from the start that metal detecting (known in the business as relic shooting) the boomtowns of Washington, or any other state, is a far more enjoyable hobby for the whole family, than it is a get-rich-quick scheme. There is still wealth in those mountains. There always was, there is now, and there will always be old rare and valuable coins, jewelry, trinkets, square nails, and artifacts resting undetected where they were lost or hidden away many years ago.

Gold and silver caches are still right where their depositors secretly buried them, for sometimes sickness, accidents, exposure, or other abrupt fatal mishaps, prevented them from being recovered by their owners. Small caches of coins fall into the same pattern, as do the fewer larger caches. Circumstances sometimes canceled any knowledge of these caches and ended any chance of recovery.

Old tobacco tins, such as this can, sometimes reveal small treasure caches.

Even so, those overgrown paths and boomtown streets are not paved with gold and silver. Perhaps this is why finding such a relic of hundred years past is so rewarding, as is the search for such items.

The Benefits of Metal Detecting

Metal detecting is an enjoyable hobby for most people. Few indeed are those lucky enough to ever find sufficient items worth enough to raise their standard of living or free them from their high-stress jobs. Metal detecting benefits your health tremendously. It improves your mental condition beyond belief. It makes a person stronger in mind and body and can be great physical therapy for you and your family. Metal detecting in boomtowns is all this, but even more specialized.

For those of you that can stand high altitudes, vigorous climbs, and the all-too-few financial rewards, this is a hobby for you. It does things for one's mental and physical being, those large sums of money could never buy. The possibility of actually finding that big gold, silver, and coin cache will always be in the back of your mind. Can any price be put on the time spent resting at the top of a steep mountain after a hike when one looks out across valleys, beyond the lakes and rivers, on past the thick forest to the snow capped mountains miles away?

For the family that wants a real challenge, dependent on one's own time and abilities, metal detecting the boomtowns offers a sport beyond compare. The limits and goals are all set by the individual. The rewards may be few or fantastic. Careful consideration and thoughtful research improves one's chances. Those of you who plan to step from your vehicle, poke around for a few minutes, and return home loaded with all sorts of "valuable relic finds" will be disappointed.

This book is for those willing to do their own thinking, researching, and exploring. I hope you will see in the abandoned boomtown sites throughout Washington a loveliness and thrilling history. It is my hope that this book will be valuable to those who truly like to explore the past and those who thrill in discovering themselves in the boomtowns where people once lived.

I would say that there are basically three different types of boomtowns. First is the community that has grown up or reestablished in or around some old boomtowns, often capitalizing on the past history and glory of the original town. Winthrop, Washington in the Methow Valley would be a prime example of a healthy community that is anything but a ghost town.

The second type of site is what most folks think of when ghost towns are mentioned. Deserted, shaky structures neglected and at the mercy of the elements and highly deserving of protection. This type should be given careful consideration. Unless you have special permission, as much as you like to treasure hunt, it can be more trouble then pleasure. A good example of this type of old boomtown would be Bodie, Washington in Okanogan County.

The third type of site, and most common, is what can be called the "bare bones" ghost town. Nature has taken over, and not much remains to show that a thriving boomtown once existed at all. A good example of this type of old mining camp would be Ruby, Washington in Okanogan County.

"Do Not Trespass"

"No Trespassing," "Keep Out," "Posted, Private Property," "Historic Site." Such signs are often all-too-common for those who would seek out and search the grounds of boomtowns. The best advice would be to FOLLOW POSTED SIGN WARNINGS, DO NOT TRESPASS.

Standing boomtowns should be worked carefully. No Trespassing signs should be strictly honored. The buildings should never be vandalized, posted or not. Treasure hunters should work diligently to make themselves a good name, for themselves individually and for the hobby field itself in whole. In actuality, the best sites to work are those where hardly a trace of the former boomtown is left. Then, one cannot be blamed for tearing down what was torn down long ago.

Totally abandoned ghost town places also have not had the severe picking-over suffered by more scenic, better known spots. Few people ever visit such desolated sites, and those who do, seeing very little, usually don't stay long.

Getting Started: The Equipment

When getting started in the hobby of metal detecting, let's keep to the basics and keep the hobby inexpensive for the family to enjoy. I would recommend a simple, turn on-and-go detector. No bells and whistles to confuse you. At a later time, after you have been with the hobby for awhile and feel comfortable with your detector, you may want to consider upgrading. A metal detector does not have to be complicated and expensive to be good. These prices were advertised at the time of publication.

Fisher 1212X: This would be the first type of detector I would recommend. You get no extras with this detector, but a lot of performance features such as: automatic VLF-ground rejection, variable trash rejection, built-in speaker, and headphone jack. Just one simple knob controls the 1212X. Set the trash rejection control, and start searching. Fisher 1212X is a sophisticated instrument that is simple enough for a child to operate. It costs less, but gives you the same high standard of Fisher quality known worldwide. Priced under $200.00. Top of the line Fisher detector, the **CZ-7aPro**, is priced around $900.00.

White's Classic SL I: This metal detector is easy to operate with built-in performance and real discrimination. Preset by the factory to handle most grounds, you can adjust it manually as well. Discriminate control with preset settings for coin and ring range. Ring range detects all jewelry, and coin range discriminates out most junk when hunting in trashy areas. Priced under $200.00. Top of the line White's detector, the **Spectrum XLT**, is priced around $700.00.

Garrett Treasure Ace 100: Don't let the low price of the Treasure Ace 100 mislead you. Remember that this is Garrett quality and performance in the field that won't let you down. Just turn it on, and its automatic ground-balancing and discrimination circuits take over. Listen for its audio alert, and dig your treasures. You'll love this little treasure finder! Priced under $200. Top of the line Garrett detector, the **GTI-2500 Pro Package**, is priced around $1,000.00

Tesoro Silver uMax: This is a detector for all ages! Fun and easy to use with a low price tag! One-knob operation lets you set the discrimination where you want it. Zero discrimination puts you in the "all metal" mode. Unique pole and handle design lets kids use the regular handle setup, while adults can attach the speed handle with arm cup. Priced under $250.00. Top of the line Tesoro detector, the **Golden uMax**, is priced around $425.00.

Other detecting equipment you would want to consider purchasing to get started would be:
1. Digging tool

2. Coil cover
3. Treasure pouch
4. A good "How to get started metal detecting" book, for example, *Let's Talk Treasure Hunting* by Charles Garrett.

Research

Where do successful treasure hunters find all those coins, rings, relics, and treasures? They find them anywhere people congregated, which is practically everywhere. One learns of these places through research. Research will help you locate the good sites and will increase the value of your old finds.

Researching a site, whether it is the boomtowns, old parks, playgrounds, and so on can be fun and exciting. Then, to locate the site and come home with your treasures is beyond belief. A good place to get started is your local library, the Internet,

This is just a small cache of the several hundred old coins and trade tokens the author has unearthed while exploring and treasure hunting throughout Northeastern Washington.

and museums. On the top of my list are local historical societies. These can be quite helpful in locating a specific boomtown in their area. Not all small towns have a historical society. Another good source would be old newspaper articles. The list is endless. Treasure found by accident represents but a small percentage of that located by persons using good research practices and techniques.

Where to Hunt

Let's keep it simple from the start. First of all, there are numerous areas around where you live that are good areas to detect. I would first start out with your local park or school. If it's a county park, you may need a metal detecting permit from your local county parks and recreation department. I have found lots of great finds at parks and schools, not necessarily always old, but of some value. Some of these items include tax tokens, old railroad trolley tokens, Indian head pennies, wheat back pennies, mercury dimes, buffalo nickels, rings, charms, necklaces, and many other valuable items.

Again, to find the older items, this is where your research will be useful. As I mentioned before, this can be a family hobby. Starting out with your new hobby of metal detecting at some of the mentioned areas will give you the opportunity to find a variety of items. This way, you will not lose interest in the hobby as you get started. It's a lot like fishing—you might think you like it, but if you're not catching fish, it's not as much fun.

In case anyone might misunderstand, there is nothing wrong with hunting parks, playgrounds, and schools. Good coins and artifacts are still being found in such locations. Old, valuable coins and jewelry still turn up in parks and such places that are supposedly "hunted out."

These are a few of the many old coins and rare trade tokens the author has recovered during his many years of treasure hunting.

TREASURE HUNTER'S CODE OF ETHICS

I **WILL** respect private property and do no treasure hunting without the owner's permission.

I **WILL** fill all excavations.

I **WILL** appreciate and protect our heritage of natural resources, wildlife, and private property.

I **WILL** use thoughtfulness, consideration, and courtesy at all times.

I **WILL** build fires in designated or safe places only.

I **WILL** leave gates as found.

I **WILL** remove and properly dispose of any trash that I find.

I **WILL** respect private and public property, all historical and archeological sites, and will do no metal detecting on these lands without proper permission.

I **WILL** keep informed on and obey all laws, regulations, and ruled governing federal, state, and local public lands.

I **WILL** observe the "Golden Rule," using outdoor manners and conducting myself at all times in a manner that will add to the stature and public image of all people engaged in the field of metal detecting.

I **WILL** not litter.

I **WILL** not destroy property, buildings, or what is left of ghost towns and deserted structures.

I **WILL** not tamper with signs, structural facilities, or equipment.

A FINAL NOTE

Without history, there would be no heritage, and only by gathering the fading old memories of yesteryear and handing them down from generation to generation can we preserve it. Neither the present nor the future can be complete without the past.

I encourage descendants of our late pioneer families that may have historic photos or recollections for other history buffs to enjoy and learn from to contact me and make them available for future publication. I feel that each story deserves to be told and recorded.

Jerry Smith
Winthrop, Washington

ORDER FORM

To order additional copies of *Boom Towns & Relic Hunters of Northeastern Washington State*, please send $19.95, plus $3.00 Shipping & Handling, to:

Jerry Smith
P.O. Box 914
Black Diamond, Washington 98010

Please make check or money order payable to Jerry Smith.

If you prefer to order additional copies through e-mail correspondence, contact Jerry@GhostTownsUSA.com or by using your MasterCard or Visa by calling *Elfin Cove Press* directly at 206-624-4544 or toll free at 1-888-465-2619.

_____ Copies @ $19.95 ea.   _____

$3.00 Shipping & Handling   _____

Washington State residents add 8.6% sales tax   _____

Total enclosed   _____

We hope you enjoy the read!

Ship To:

Name _____

Address _____

City _____

State _____ Zip Code_____